THEY MADE A REVOLUTION
The Sons and Daughters of the American Revolution

"Sure to be one of many comparable retrospectives . . . and one of the more appealing."

—Kirkus Reviews

THEY MADE A REVOLUTION

THE SONS AND DAUGHTERS
OF THE AMERICAN REVOLUTION

Jules Archer
History for Young Readers

THEY MADE A REVOLUTION

THE SONS AND DAUGHTERS OF THE AMERICAN REVOLUTION

JULES ARCHER
Foreword by Kathleen Krull

Sky Pony Press

NEW YORK

35847754

Historical texts often reflect the time period in which they were written, and new information is constantly being discovered. This book was originally published in 1973, and much has changed since then. While every effort has been made to bring this book up to date, it is important to consult multiple sources when doing research.

Sky Pony Press books may be purchased in bulk at special discounts for sales promotion, corporate gifts, fund-raising, or educational purposes. Special editions can also be created to specifications. For details, contact the Special Sales Department, Sky Pony Press, 307 West 36th Street, 11th Floor, New York, NY 10018 or info@skyhorsepublishing.com.

Sky Pony® is a registered trademark of Skyhorse Publishing, Inc.®, a Delaware corporation.

Visit our website at www.skyponypress.com.

10 9 8 7 6 5 4 3 2 1

Library of Congress Cataloging-in-Publication Data is available on file.

Print ISBN: 978-1-63450-195-8
Ebook ISBN: 978-1-63450-626-7

Series design by Brian Peterson
Cover photo credit Library of Congress

Printed in the United States of America

CONTENTS

FOREWORD

This clever collective biography was first published under a slightly different title as a Scholastic paperback in 1973—probably timed as a lead-in to the gala 200th anniversary of America's birth. That was Jules Archer's claim to fame: if you needed a book for young readers about history—say, the resistance movement of 1776—he was the man.

Archer pulls us into the year 1776 with portraits of ten of the principal actors of the American Revolution. He focuses on personalities, warts and all, allowing us to get to know these heroes as human beings. He freely uses their letters and diaries to reveal their everyday struggles, as they gradually become aware of how they are influencing history.

These aren't complete life stories, however. Instead, in an ingenious structure, he shows how each person's life led to one very specific, thrilling moment: June 7, 1776. On that fateful day, forward-thinking Richard Henry Lee of Virginia stood up and declared to his fellow Congressmen that the thirteen colonies being governed by England should be "free and independent states."

An illegal bombshell of a proposal, and one that could have gotten him and his listeners hanged for treason. Indeed, Archer injects suspense right from the second page. To England, these men were traitors of the first order, and this was a battle cry. And if it did come to war? The outcome was unpredictable and could have been catastrophic, death, and destruction for all. If anything, the chances of winning against the most powerful nation on earth were slim to none.

Imagine the tension, imagine the courage of these first American patriots.

Archer uses catchy chapter titles to highlight each one. "The Cranky Yankee"—that's John Adams all over. He was obnoxious, unpopular (and he knew it), but the one who seconded Lee's motion and was absolutely indispensable to the new nation. In "The Sly Fox," we can read about cagey Sam Adams in action, rabble-rousing Bostonians into revolt. "The Rich Rebel" brings John Hancock to life, serving the finest wines, dashing about town in coats embroidered with gold, risking his fortune to support Sam Adams, utterly devoted to the cause.

There's the "The Thunder Master"—the always-mesmerizing Benjamin Franklin. "The Silent Redhead" gives us a new way of looking at Thomas Jefferson—besides examining his hair, we see him as the second-youngest man in Congress, one who hardly ever spoke unless he truly had something to say. "The Disgusted General" makes us feel both sorrow and admiration for George Washington. He started from the bottom as a teenage surveyor crawling in the mud, was already a major in the Virginia militia by nineteen, and rose to the very top, never saying no when asked to serve his country.

"The Silver-Tongued Bumpkin" is Patrick Henry—an odd duck with an odd accent. But by all accounts he was the most spellbinding speaker ever, electrifying listeners with his "give me liberty . . . or give me death!" Thomas Paine is "The Man of Common Sense," a recent immigrant who changed thousands of minds, including George Washington's, with his pamphlet, *Common Sense*, calling for independence.

As for the "daughters" of the American Revolution, Archer strikes a contemporary note by going out of his way to mention women. He includes two separate chapters on the very brave Abigail Adams and full-of-secrets Martha Washington, giving each woman her due as an activist, motivator, advisor, and patriot. Another chapter talks up the fighter known as Mollie Pitcher; Deborah Samson, who served three years as a soldier; and several others. Archer makes clear that women were vital to the resistance movement.

He adds another modern tone in discussing what each of his heroes thought about slavery—how most considered it morally wrong, with even the ones who had slaves experiencing seriously conflicted feelings. The banning of slavery was actually in the Declaration of Independence at first, then got dropped, with many mourning the injustice to black Americans and predicting what it would take to get rid of the evil institution.

Following his portraits of the patriots, Archer has chapters on the twenty-seven days of tortured debate that followed Lee's proposal, the birth of the Declaration of Independence and a little about the fifty-six men who signed it, and a wrapping-up of what happened to everyone afterward.

As for quibbles: in his efforts to humanize these figures we know mostly as marble statues, Archer leans on clichés of physical description and the occasional dated phrase. In general, he's a little too dismissive of Martha Washington, downplaying her smarts—she was well-read. Based on my own research (for *A Kids' Guide to the First Ladies*, HarperCollins, 2017), he makes too much of George's first love, Sally Fairfax, and the pall she supposedly cast over his marriage. There's plenty of evidence that

George and Martha couldn't have been more devoted to each other. Likewise, there is proof that Paul Revere did not make Washington's dentures, as Archer says. The story that Archer tells may go deeper than history, but he gives us accessible stories and characters, breathing life into history. Were Archer writing this today, he'd have included back matter—bibliography, an index, and especially sources for quotes.

But he does succeed in synthesizing great gobs of history into a succinct account of this world-changing drama. As *Kirkus Reviews* pointed out at the time, this book was "sure to be one of many comparable retrospectives . . . and one of the more appealing." Jules Archer has given us a compelling, compact volume about the personalities who shaped our country—one well worth discussing in classrooms today.

—Kathleen Krull

ONE

Who Were They?

The Founding Fathers and Mothers of our country were not, as history texts often make them seem, stuffy cardboard figures of unbelievable virtue and nobility. They were, of course, emotional, flesh-and-blood people with no lack of human weaknesses. But they were caught up in the excitement of turbulent times that led many of them to risk their necks in a desperate determination to resist tyranny.

This book tells what the leading Americans in that resistance movement were really like, as deduced from their letters, diaries, and reminiscences, up to the moment they openly declared revolution. They gambled that they could persuade Americans to stick together and fight hard enough, and long enough, to force the mightiest nation in the world of 1776 to let them secede from the British Empire.

Their chances of winning that gamble, they knew, were slim. It was far more likely that the British would hang them as traitors, devastate the colonies, and leave their children weeping in the ruins.

"What do we mean by the revolution?" asked John Adams, reflecting as an old man of eighty. "The war with Britain? That was no part of the revolution; it was only the effect and consequence of it. The revolution was in the minds and hearts of the people, and this was effected from 1760 to 1775, in the course of fifteen years, before a drop of blood was shed at Lexington."

Not all the great patriots of '76 were signers of the Declaration of Independence. Many were not at the Second Continental Congress to sign it but, like Washington and Patrick Henry, were busy working elsewhere for Independence. No woman signed, but the spirits of Abigail Adams, Martha Washington, and Martha Jefferson unquestionably left a unique imprint on the birth of freedom.

We first meet and get to know each patriot up to the crucial day in his or her life—June 7, 1776—when Richard Henry Lee of Virginia stood up at the Congress to propose that the United Colonies "are, and of right ought to be, free and independent States." We then watch those at the Congress fighting bitterly over Independence for the twenty-seven feverish days that followed. Final chapters tell of the signers of the Declaration, and what happened to them afterwards.

Here, then, are the hearts and minds of those bold men and women of 1776 who didn't hang, because they won their desperate gamble to be free.

TWO

The Sly Fox:

Sam Adams

Sam Adams's wife told him about the valuable present a relative was sending them—a slave girl. He hit the roof.

"A slave cannot live in *my* house!" he roared. "If she comes, she must be free!" And free she was, just as he was determined all Americans must be.

"If it were revealed to me that 999 Americans out of 1,000 would perish in a war for liberty," he told patriot Dr. Benjamin Rush, "I would vote for that war, rather than see my country enslaved."

He was a seedy failure who almost went to jail for being seven thousand pounds short in his funds as tax collector. As leader of the radical Whig Party, he devoted himself night and day to manufacturing a revolution instead of making money. A master of propaganda, he was wholly unscrupulous, using any means to justify his ends. He built the Sons of Liberty into a violent subversive movement. His talent for magnifying grievances into protest rallies, like the uproar he created over what he labeled the "Boston Massacre," led more respectable Americans to shun him as a rabble-rouser.

He was born in Boston on September 27, 1722. His father, a brewer, was active in the movement to win more self-rule for the colonists of Massachusetts. Sam grew up inspired by the fiery debates he heard at meetings in his home.

Fellow students at Harvard found him an intelligent, modest, pleasant fellow, although no saint. He had to pay a fine for tippling rum, and was chastised for oversleeping when he was due in chapel. His education was threatened when his father lost his money, but Sam managed to stay at Harvard by waiting on tables in the dining hall.

Graduating in 1740, he tried his hand at several business ventures but failed. It was hardly surprising, because he was constantly up to his ears in politics. He lost no opportunity to stir up public anger against the royal Governor or the British Parliament. But twenty-six-year-old Sam insisted that the authorities were the real rebels, not him. They were in rebellion against "the undoubted rights and liberties of the people." The colonists had the right, Sam said, to question their conduct when it favored the King instead of the Americans.

He managed to eke out a threadbare existence when he was elected tax collector for Boston in 1756. Kindhearted, easygoing, and sympathetic, he could never bring himself to press tax delinquents to pay up. Besides, he was too involved in politics to bother. Worse, he was so often broke that some tax funds trickled into his own pockets.

After eight years he was found to be seven thousand pounds short in his accounts. There was angry talk of prosecuting him. But Sam shrewdly got Bostonians so mad about the stamp tax that they forgot about the scandal and elected him to the Massachusetts House of Representatives.

Most colonial politicians were well-to-do men who did not have to depend on the slim salaries of public office. Sam did, and remained a poor man all his life because of his dedication to the dream of self-rule.

Although he kept insisting that the colonists were suffering intolerable oppression under the Crown, most Americans, in fact, were satisfied and considered themselves patriotic Britons. Their chief complaint was not too different from that of most Americans today—increasing taxes and the unfair way in which they were levied.

Sam seized this issue to fan the flames of popular indignation. Making the rounds of the Boston taverns, he built up cells of opposition. These grew into angry patriot clubs and secret societies, which began spreading through New England. Tories contemptuously called the troublemaker "Sam the Publican" (innkeeper). The Boston taverns were the true cradle of the American Revolution, and Sam was their political boss.

He wasn't much of a public speaker, because his voice quavered and his hands shook from palsy.

But he was a superb conspirator who loved to manipulate people and events from behind the scenes. He wrote inflammatory speeches for Whig orators, organized oppositions to the Crown at town meetings, sent protest letters to the papers, and stirred up mobs to violence. He even trained his large mongrel, Queue, to bite and maul British soldiers attached to Boston regiments.

Untidy and indifferent about his dress, Sam nevertheless had a warm personality that charmed people and made him a thousand friends in all walks of life. He enjoyed loafing and joking with them on the wharves, on the Common and, of course, in the taverns. Although devoutly religious, he never behaved in a holier-than-thou manner.

When Parliament passed the sugar tax in 1764, Sam called it an illegal act. If Americans let England get away with it, he warned, Parliament would begin taxing everything else the colonists used or owned. The storm he raised compelled the colony's legislators to petition for repeal of the Sugar Act.

Now forty-two, he married a second time, his first wife having died seven years earlier, leaving him with two small children on his hands. Betsy Welles, his second wife, proved to be just the kind of skillful, economical home manager the improvident Sam needed. But he treasured her even more because she enthusiastically encouraged his tweaking of the King's nose.

Sam, Betsy, and the children said prayers before meals and read the Bible at bedtime. Sam also organized hymn-singing societies. But Lt. Governor Thomas Hutchinson noted sourly that Sam's hymn singers invariably turned up in the anti-Crown demonstrations he organized. Calling his Puritanism a mask for radicalism, Hutchinson accused Sam of using Boston's churches as political soapboxes to "sound the yell of rebellion in the ears of an ignorant and deluded people."

The sugar tax was followed by the Stamp Act of 1765, requiring a tax to be paid for official seals on all newspapers and legal and commercial documents. But businessmen, mechanics, and laborers in New England were already complaining about hard times. Making the rounds of the Green Dragon, the Bunch of Grapes and other taverns, Sam Adams lost no opportunity to persuade them that the fault was all England's.

Calling the Stamp Act a crisis for Americans that cried out for resistance, he won election to the Massachusetts House of Representatives to fight it. Within two weeks he was on every important committee. In the summer of 1765 he organized a secret society called the Sons of Liberty, dedicated to sabotaging enforcement of the Stamp Act.

Among his recruits were his young country cousin, lawyer John Adams; silversmith Paul Revere; influential Boston physician Joseph Warren; and, most important of all, merchant John Hancock, one of Boston's wealthiest young men.

Sam distrusted Hancock as a vacillating peacock, but valued his money to finance the Sons. It didn't hurt Sam's influence, either, to have behind him a noted businessman who provided jobs for a thousand New England workers in his various enterprises. And when Sam was drowning in personal bills, he could count on Hancock's purse to come to his rescue.

It was also open to him when he cultivated Andrew Mcintosh, an illiterate thug who led a gang of waterfront toughs, and Adams used them for rioting when it served his purpose. Making peace between them and a rival gang they often fought with, Sam convinced both to fight instead on the same side against the common enemy, British tax collectors.

On August 14th Sam used his private army of the Sons of Liberty, aided by Mcintosh's ruffians, to frighten those who sought to enforce the Stamp Act. Stamp headquarters was smashed by a mob who hung an effigy of Andrew Oliver, the Crown official in charge, on an oak known as "the Liberty Tree." The effigy was then taken down, carried to Oliver's house and beheaded. When some Sons broke in, vowing to kill him, Oliver fled in panic. He resigned the next day.

Sam was delighted by the success of his ruse. The day "ought to be for ever remembered in America," he exulted, because "the People shouted; and their shout was heard to the distant end of this continent." The *Boston Gazette* noted, "The resistance of that day roused the spirit of America."

Mob rule reigned in Boston for three days. At Sam's instigation another mob smashed into and looted the house of Lt. Governor Hutchinson, who was Oliver's brother-in-law. Adams had shown Americans, not only in Boston, but throughout the thirteen colonies, that if they were bold enough they could defy the King, Parliament, and all unjust tax laws.

Nine colonies took the cue, organizing a Stamp Act Congress that branded the act as illegal "taxation without consent," and demanded its repeal. Their "Declaration of Rights and Grievances" had sympathizers in Parliament. They won.

The news brought great rejoicing in the colonies. Sam was thrilled with his victory, but soon grew glum. "The repeal of the Stamp Act," noted his cousin John, "has hushed into silence almost every popular clamor, and composed every wave of popular disorder into a smooth and peaceful calm."

Sam's Whig party, also known as the People's party, Liberty party, or Country party, lost members rapidly. He tried to whip up new radical fervor with propaganda, and organized noisy Sons of Liberty parades and fireworks to celebrate repeal of the Stamp Act. The Tories confidently ignored his mobs as "rabble" and "scum." Without fresh provocation from London, Sam knew, his cause would wither and die.

It was saved, ironically, by the originator of the Stamp Act, Richard Grenville, who was outraged when Parliament repealed it. Rising in the House of Commons, he sneered at his fellow members,

"You are cowards! You are afraid of the Americans—you dare not tax America!"

Charles Townshend, Britain's treasurer, grew indignant. "Cowards? Dare not tax America? Dare tax America!"

"Dare you? I wish to God I could see it!"

"I will, I will!" Townshend exploded. And that was how and why new taxes were levied against America under the Townshend Acts, which gave Sam Adams the fuel he desperately needed to keep the fires of freedom burning.

When the colonists were compelled to pay duties on glass, lead, paints, paper, and tea they imported from England, Sam led a boycott movement on all British goods. The Sons of Liberty pressured American merchants to sign a pledge of "nonimportation." When eight Boston merchants broke the pledge, Sam decided to make an example of one of them.

One of his mobs gathered in front of the store of Theophilus Lilly with a big wooden hand on a pole pointing to it accusingly. A friend of Lilly's sought to wrest the pole away, and was beaten up. Enraged, he secured his musket and fired into the crowd, killing 11-year-old Christopher Snyder.

Sam promptly arranged a big public funeral with the coffin, inscribed "Innocence itself is not safe," on display in front of the Liberty Tree. In the *Boston Gazette* he inflamed angry citizens further by describing young Chris Snyder as "the first martyr to American liberty."

Now clerk of the Massachusetts legislature, Sam wrote its stinging reproaches to King George and his ministers. In February 1768 he drew up the Massachusetts Circular Letter sent to the other twelve colonies, urging united opposition to the Crown by discussion and petition. Horrified, Governor Francis Bernard denounced it as seditious.

At times Sam seemed to worry that he might go too far or too fast. He let the Sons of Liberty surround the houses of the royal Customs Commissioners at night, beating drums, blowing horns, and uttering bloodcurdling Indian war whoops. But he warned them to avoid violence now, for fear of losing the sympathetic support of other colonies.

"We know who have abused us . . . but let not the hair of their scalps be touched," he told his followers. "The time is coming when they shall, like the dust, melt away."

But the frightened Commissioners appealed to London for protection. Several regiments of British troops were rushed to Boston from Halifax. News that they were on their way provided Sam with a golden opportunity.

"We will destroy every soldier that dares put foot on shore!" he cried at a town meeting. "His Majesty has no right to send troops here to invade the country, and I look upon them as foreign enemies!" He agitated the people of Boston in the streets, shipyards, shops, and taverns.

But British troops under General Thomas Gage took possession of Boston without firing a shot.

Sam and his followers became objects of derision in other colonies.

Sam angrily urged every Bostonian to arm himself with a flintlock to oppose "the enemy." To avoid arrest for treason, he pretended to be talking about "an approaching war with France," but everybody knew what he meant. He appealed to Bostonians not to let Redcoats stop them on the streets and force them to identify themselves.

"To be called to account by a common soldier, or any soldier," he wrote wrathfully in the *Gazette,* "is a badge of slavery which none but a slave will wear!"

One day Sam went too far. Haranguing a crowd, he cried, "If you are men, behave like men! Let us take up arms immediately and be free and seize all the King's officers. We shall have thirty thousand men to join us from the country. . . . We will not submit to any tax nor become slaves. We will take up arms and spend our last drop of blood before the King and Parliament shall impose on us!"

It was America's first call to revolution—eight years before the Declaration of Independence. Lt. Governor Hutchinson indignantly sought to indict Sam for sedition, but a Boston grand jury refused. Hutchinson wrote angry letters to a friend in Parliament, warning that the Crown had better crack down on agitators like Adams before it was too late.

Friends who passed Sam's house after midnight often saw the lamp still lit in his study, and knew that he was hard at work writing against the Tories—inflammatory letters, essays, documents. Betsy frequently fell asleep to the "lullaby" of her husband's quill scratching in the next room.

At forty-eight, Sam's forehead was deeply furrowed, brows sticking out beyond the corners of his clear gray eyes. A long, full nose protruded over a determined chin. His dress was Spartan—a patched tailcoat, shabby waistcoat, a show of threadbare white linen at the throat, homespun breeches, wool stockings, shoes with scratched brass buckles. He wore no wig under his tricorne hat, and brushed his thinning gray hair straight back.

His expression was deceptively mild and his voice good-natured, until he delivered an angry speech. Then, said an American Tory painter, "If I wished to draw a picture of the Devil, I would want no better model than Sam Adams."

London felt compelled to recall Governor Bernard, replacing him with Hutchinson. To humiliate Bernard, Sam had the Sons of Liberty celebrate his departure with bells, cannonfire and huge bonfires. Word now came that the unpopular Townshend Acts were likely to be repealed. Determined not to let popular unrest die down, Sam set about provoking a riot that would freshly inflame Americans.

On March 5, 1770, he goaded one of his waterfront mobs into taunting and stoning Redcoats guarding the Boston Custom House. The soldiers opened fire, killing or mortally wounding five civilians. Sam promptly labeled the clash "the

Boston Massacre," and succeeded in infuriating all the colonies over this "military outrage" against "peace-loving citizens."

He forced a trial of the soldiers, and kept passions stirred by melodramatic references to Boston dogs "greedily licking human BLOOD in King Street." He arranged to have March 5th set aside as an annual day of mourning with tolling bells, lighted picture displays of the "horrid Massacre," and rabble-rousing oratory. His agitation spurred all colonies to build and train their own militia for "defense."

Having united the colony behind him, the leader of American opposition to the Crown sought to unite all the colonies behind Massachusetts. For this purpose Sam linked them with Committees of Correspondence he set up to spread word of Crown attempts to curb American liberties, and to discuss how best to defeat these attempts.

In June 1773 Sam saw a golden opportunity to discredit Governor Hutchinson and, by inference, all royal governors in the colonies. The letters Hutchinson had written to London urging that troops be sent to enforce tax collections fell into Benjamin Franklin's hands there, and Franklin sent them directly to the Massachusetts Whigs.

Sam read them aloud to the legislature, emphasizing Hutchinson's opinion that it was absurd for Englishmen overseas to expect to enjoy the same liberties as Englishmen at home.

"The plan for the ruin of American liberty," Sam cried, "was laid by a few men born and educated amongst us, and governed by avarice and a lust for power!" He published the letters in all the colonies through the Committees of Correspondence, and they created a sensation.

To placate the colonists, Parliament had repealed all import duties under the Townshend Acts except the tax on tea. That ended the boycott on British goods. But Sam was determined to continue agitating over the tea tax. In December 1773, when Hutchinson let two tea ships sail into Boston harbor, Sam rang meeting-house bells throughout the city to call a huge town meeting of protest.

He led several thousand Bostonians to demand the tea ships be ordered to return to London. A delegation returned to report Hutchinson's refusal. Sam shouted, "This meeting can do nothing more to save the country!" It was a prearranged signal. A mob of his followers, disguised as Mohawk Indians, rushed to the waterfront crying, "Boston Harbor a teapot tonight!"

Boarding the tea ships, they worked all night dumping 343 chests of tea into the harbor. One of the "Indians," George Hewes, later identified Sam and John Hancock as having helped him lift and tip several chests. Afterwards Sam wrote the Committees of Correspondence that the Boston Tea Party had been a "glorious illegality" essential to avoid "abject slavery."

"The die is now cast," wrote King George angrily to Lord North. "The Colonies must either submit or triumph."

If rebellious Boston was not punished, the King and Parliament were convinced, then other colonies would quickly decide to challenge British authority. So the port of Boston was closed to all commerce until the Americans paid for the tea.

To signify that Massachusetts was now under military rule, General Thomas Gage was made the new governor. The Crown sent him several regiments, and Bostonians were forced to quarter the troops.

Sam sped Paul Revere off to other colonies to plead for their help against these "Intolerable Acts." He warned them, "You will be called upon to surrender all your rights, if ever they should succeed in their attempts to suppress the spirit of liberty *here.*" But the merchants of other colonies were upset by Sam's demand that they strike back by once again imposing a boycott on all British goods.

The furthest the Committees of Correspondence would go was to plan a Continental Congress to petition Parliament for a redress of grievances, and decide together what to do next if it was denied. Sam was forced to go along, although by now he felt the crisis called for rebellion, not petitions.

Sam kept the plan secret from General Gage, so that the Governor would not close the legislature before Sam could arrange an election of delegates. One day in June 1774, exercising his authority as Clerk of the House, he suddenly locked the doors of the assembly and proposed the appointment of five delegates, including John Adams and himself, to the Continental Congress meeting in Philadelphia in September.

Sam's friends worried that he would create a bad impression at the Congress because he had only a few sloppy, threadbare suits. So with John Hancock footing the bill, he was forced into a tailor shop for a new wardrobe. When he set out for Philadelphia with the other Massachusetts delegates, it was the first time in his life that the fifty-two-year-old man had ever been that far beyond Boston.

It was something of a shock for him when he met the delegates from other colonies, most of them well-to-do and aristocratic, especially those from the South. Sam, a poor man and a thoroughgoing democrat, was looked upon as something of a low-class rabble-rouser, not really fit for the company of gentlemen. In order not to antagonize these well-bred, well-dressed gentlemen, Sam changed his style. The Virginians were impressed with the quiet reasonableness he now displayed.

But Pennsylvanian Joseph Galloway, leader of the Congress conservatives, saw Sam as a sly fox trying to stampede the delegates into rash actions against the Crown. He accused Sam of ordering his Boston patriots to stir up trouble and force General Gage to order out troops, whereupon Sons of Liberty express riders would fly to Philadelphia with the news, in order to excite the Congress.

"He eats little, drinks little, sleeps little, thinks much," grumbled Galloway, "and is most decisive and indefatigable in the pursuit of his objects." When he denounced Sam's proposal "to eat nothing, drink nothing, wear nothing" imported from England, he received threats against his life. One note said, "Hang yourself or we shall do it for you!" Galloway blamed Sam and the Philadelphia Sons of Liberty.

After a little over seven weeks, the First Continental Congress adjourned on October 26, 1774. Returning home, Sam threw himself into the task of organizing a Massachusetts army of eighteen thousand "Minutemen," a militia of patriots pledged to assemble at a minute's notice to fight the Redcoats if they went outside Boston. This was the last straw for the Crown, which put a price on the heads of Sam Adams and John Hancock as outlaws. The two patriots fled to hide at Lexington, where General Gage sent troops to search for them. Warned by Paul Revere, they escaped and left for Philadelphia and the Second Continental Congress.

When it opened on May 10, 1775, Sam worked diligently behind the scenes to convince the delegates that the Redcoats' attacks on the Minutemen at Lexington and Concord—"the shot heard 'round the world"—had made it impossible for Americans to remain British any longer. The Battle of Bunker Hill in June gave Sam fresh ammunition to urge independence.

Worried about his wife Betsy, he wrote her, "It is painful to me to reflect on the terror I must suppose you were under on hearing the noise of war so near you." She replied that she hadn't been a bit frightened. A letter from one of Sam's friends told him that Betsy had been "steady and calm under trial."

Sam was startled when a British colonel came to Philadelphia to see him on a secret mission from General Gage. If Sam would end his opposition to the Government and make his peace with the King, the colonel revealed, he would be pardoned and offered numerous personal benefits.

"No personal considerations shall ever induce me to abandon the righteous cause of my country!" Sam exploded indignantly, showing the colonel the door. "And tell Governor Gage that it is the advice of Samuel Adams to him no longer to insult the feelings of an exasperated people!"

In August King George had Sam in mind when he accused the Americans, "misled by dangerous and ill-designing men, and forgetting the allegiance which they owe to the power that has protected and supported them," of "traitorously preparing, ordering, and levying war against us." He intended, he warned grimly, to "bring the traitors to justice."

By October word arrived from England that the King had not only refused to read the Congress's petition of grievances, but in Parliament had proclaimed the Americans to be rebels who would be put down by force.

"The tyrant!" Sam exploded. "His speech breathes the most malevolent spirit, and determines my opinion of its author as a man of wicked heart!" But many delegates were frightened and anxious to assure the Crown that they had no intention of rebelling as Sam wanted. They were convinced that the King was sending commissioners with a peace proposal. But no commissioners arrived even by spring.

Meanwhile Sam's long struggle to break the colonies away from England began to bear fruit as more and more delegates were won over by his arguments. He persuaded John Adams that the cause of Independence would become more respectable if they stayed in the background and let the highly regarded "gentlemen of Virginia" propose it.

Then, on June 7, 1776, Richard Henry Lee rose in the Congress to propose a stirring resolution that the United Colonies "are, and of right ought to be, free and independent States."

W. G. Evelyn, an outraged British officer with Howe's forces, wrote home his disgust with sly fox Sam Adams:

"Would you believe it, that this immense continent from New England to Georgia is moved and directed by one man—a man of ordinary birth and desperate fortune, who by his abilities and talent for factional intrigue, has made himself of some consequence . . . and who must sink into insignificancy and beggary the moment it ceases?"

Thomas Jefferson put it differently.

He called Sam Adams "truly the Man of the Revolution."

THREE

The Cranky Yankee:
John Adams

Only after a stormy battle in the Continental Congress did John Adams succeed in getting a majority of delegates to agree to send to England a blistering indictment of King George that he had written. Joseph Hawley, a radical friend, wrote from Boston asking John what good it was, since it did not have the total support of the Congress. "What is your Congress doing?" Hawley demanded in disgust. "Is it dozing, amusing itself?"

"Remember," John wrote back testily, "no matter how you set them, you can't make thirteen clocks strike precisely alike!"

He had no illusions about the popularity of Independence. In 1775 he observed gloomily, "At least a third of the two million and some people living in the thirteen colonies are opposed to the Revolution, and to the whole idea of Independence."

But he was positive that those who opposed Independence were absolutely wrong, and he never stopped yelling at them that they were idiots not to see it. A cranky, crusty, self-righteous man, John Adams was stubbornly convinced that he was always right. But he had sense enough to know that he was too dour to occupy a beloved place in history like other popular patriots he envied—Washington, Jefferson, Franklin.

"Mausoleums, statues, monuments will never be erected to me," he once sighed. "Panegyrical romances will never be written, nor flattering oration spoken to transmit me to posterity in brilliant colors." For that reason, he predicted with wounded vanity, "the whole history of this Revolution will be a lie, from beginning to end."

The history books would insist, he grumbled, that "Franklin did this, Franklin did that, Franklin did some other damned thing. . . . Franklin smote the ground and out sprang George Washington, fully grown and on his horse. . . . Franklin then electrified him with his miraculous lightning rod and the three of them—Franklin, Washington, and the horse—conducted the entire Revolution by themselves."

Franklin, in turn, called John "always an honest man, often a wise one, but sometimes, and in some things, absolutely out of his senses."

A farmer's son, John Adams was born in Braintree (now Quincy), Massachusetts, on October 19, 1735. By fifteen he was a sturdy lad with blazing blue eyes and light brown hair who enjoyed life in Braintree so much that he wanted only to remain there as a farmer. He loved to hunt, sail, play ball, pitch horseshoes, go to barn dances and huskings, and run after girls. His parents were chagrined when he decided against going to Harvard to study for the clergy.

His father then proceeded to give him a taste of what farm work was really like. He kept John by his side from dawn to dusk scything hay, cleaning out the cow barn, digging a water pond, and doing other hard jobs that left the young teenager utterly exhausted. John was soon convinced that buckling down with books at Harvard would be a lot easier on his back.

Accepted there at sixteen, John divided his time between studying religion and studying girls. "I was of an amorous disposition," he admitted in his autobiography. ". . . . And very early, from ten or eleven years of age, was very fond of the society of females. I had my favorites among the young women, and spent many of my evenings in their company. . . ."

Upon graduation John decided against the clergy and ended up a struggling lawyer. Marrying Abigail Smith, a minister's daughter, he commuted to work in Boston by horseback from their little farm in Braintree.

His cousin Sam, thirteen years older than John, persuaded him to join the underground resistance against the British as a legal advocate. Awed by Sam's prestige as a leading citizen, John always insisted that he was not "the famous Adams," but only his cousin's "creature and kinsman."

When the Stamp Act was passed, Sam's call for a boycott of stamps put John in an awkward bind. Since no legal business could be transacted without stamps, a boycott meant closed courts and lawyers out of jobs. Abby expected a baby in a month, and John needed money badly.

Nevertheless, he wrote a stirring tract to arouse the people to resist the Stamp Act. When the Townshend Acts were passed, Sam asked thirty-two-year-old John to stir public protest by making a rabble-rousing speech at the town meeting. John refused. He was convinced that the new taxes ought to be resisted, but he was no revolutionary like his cousin. He deplored the idea of mob violence and rebellion, believing in English law. He simply wanted justice, not independence, from England. So he wrote legal tracts attacking taxation without representation.

In 1768 John Hancock's sloop, the *Liberty*, was seized for smuggling in a cargo of fine wines without paying duty. When Hancock asked him to fight the case, John set out to prove that the Townshend Acts were illegal and thus did not have to be obeyed. Fearful that he could do it, Governor Bernard sent his attorney general, Jonathan Sewall, John's former Harvard classmate, to get John off the case and out of the People's party by offering him the job of Advocate General in the Admiralty Court. It was an open door to power and fortune.

"I cannot in honor or conscience accept it," John said.

When he told Abby what a stubborn fool he had been, she observed, "It is a bribe, of course. A very high bribe . . . you could become Chief Justice." Then she kissed her husband, her eyes sparkling warmly with pride. "My friend, my partner, they say you are an ambitious man. Is it not something of a satisfaction to be feared by the powerful?"

He felt guilty about spending so much time on the people's cause, neglecting his work and family. "I must avoid politics, political clubs, town meetings, General Court, etc., etc.," he reproached himself in his diary. "I must spend my evenings in my office or with my family." But after the Boston Massacre he shouldered a musket and bayonet to stand watch with fellow citizens until dawn, to prevent further clashes between troops and civilians. When he came home frozen with cold, Abby would serve him a hot drink and rub his ears to warm them.

The uproar created by Sam Adams compelled the Crown to prosecute the soldiers involved in the Massacre, to avoid having them lynched by Sam's inflamed mobs. A Boston Tory appealed to John to defend them, vowing that Captain Preston, commander of the guards, was innocent, and that his soldiers had fired only to protect their lives from the mob.

John was begged to take the case because no other Boston lawyer dared risk public wrath by doing so. He did not hesitate. If he believed in anything, he believed in justice under the law—

for all, including those hated by the citizens. Was that not, after all, the very lesson the radicals were trying to teach Parliament?

"Passion and prejudice are not admissible in a court of law," he replied. "If Captain Preston thinks he cannot have a fair trial without my help, then he shall have it."

Reprisals were swift in coming. Angry citizens cried out on the street that he had forgotten to wear his red coat. One threw a mudball at him. Windows of his house were broken.

John did not become more popular by getting the officer and most of his men acquitted. Only two soldiers were found guilty of a lesser charge of manslaughter, and were released after being branded on the thumb as punishment. Other than expenses, John asked for and received no fee. Worn out, his own affairs sadly neglected, he resolved, "I shall certainly . . . become more retired and cautious; I shall certainly mind my own farm and my own business."

But Sam persuaded him to stand for election as Boston's representative to the General Court (Massachusetts Senate), even though John protested that he was too unpopular to win an election as dogcatcher. To his surprise, he won an overwhelming vote, partly because of Sam's influence, partly because of respect for John's outstanding legal talents.

But Hutchinson, now Governor, vetoed John's name because of signed articles John had written in the *Gazette* attacking Crown attempts to control the courts by paying judges' salaries. A delegation from the Massachusetts assembly sympathized with John for this check to his career.

"Check?" he exploded. "By my soul . . . I take pride in it. The Governor's veto is no check but a boost!"

He was right. Labeled an enemy of the Crown in the Governor's eyes, John automatically became a patriotic hero in the eyes of his fellow colonists. His role as Captain Preston's trial defender was now seen as an act of principle.

Sam's Boston Tea Party was much too illegal an affair for the law-abiding John Adams to join. But he admired the enterprise. He wondered what Parliament would do about it. "Will they punish us? How? By quartering troops upon us? . . . Restraining our trade?" These speculations in his diary were verified when Boston Harbor was blockaded to starve the city into submission.

Many colonies rushed help. Christopher Gadsden sent a shipment of rice from the planters of Carolina, urging Bostonians, "Don't pay for an ounce of the damned tea!"

When Bostonians were forced to quarter troops sent to subdue them, John, quivering with rage and indignation, called a meeting of patriots at Faneuil Hall. All agreed not to pay a cent for the destroyed tea, and voted unanimously to strike back by a new embargo on all British goods.

When John was elected a delegate to the First Continental Congress, he wrote with uncharacteristic modesty, "This will be an assembly of the wisest men upon the continent, who are Americans in principle. I feel myself unequal to this business." Jonathan Sewall warned him that if he went to the Congress, his career would be ruined forever.

"Britain will never alter her system," John replied. "And by that same token we shall not alter ours. I have crossed over my river. . . . Sink or swim, live or die, survive or perish—I am with my country from this day on!"

Reaching Philadelphia, the Massachusetts delegates were taken in hand by local Sons of Liberty with a warning. John wrote Abby, "'You must not,' they said, 'utter the word Independence nor give the least hint or insinuation of the idea, either in Congress or any private conversation. If you do, you are undone. . . . You are thought to be too warm, too zealous. . . . You must be therefore very cautious, you must pretend not to take the lead.'"

When Peyton Randolph of Virginia, President of the Congress, took the chair and ordered the doors locked, the delegates opened their proceedings with a pledge of secrecy. The pledge was quickly violated by almost all delegates in the coffeehouses, and in letters home to wives, friends, and provincial officials.

John found the Southerners to be the peacocks of the Congress, dressing in greens, golds, brocades, and laces, while the Puritan radicals of New England presented sober appearances in brown or black clothes of coarse cloth or linen. The contrast, however, did not prevent Sam Adams from winning friends easily, especially among the Virginians, while John felt sorely out of place. Now thirty-nine, plump, round-faced, snub-nosed, and bald, he cut an unimpressive figure at first.

Although delegates learned to respect his honesty, forthright bluntness, and keen intelligence, they liked his ill-tempered arrogance no more than had his fellow Bostonians. John admitted that he was "obnoxious, suspected and unpopular in the eyes of most members." He envied Sam's winning personality, and even sought to imitate his cousin's charm.

He found the Congress split between a majority of conservatives who aimed at patching up the quarrel with England, and a minority of radicals determined upon resistance. Strong sectional jealousies often put the delegates more in opposition to each other than to the British Crown.

The Southerners, even some Virginians, found the New Englanders' social views distasteful. Mostly aristocrats, they felt that a gentleman, who was always a gentleman, and a "lower class" person must each keep to his station, each recognizing the distinction between them. New Englanders were too full of the "leveling spirit" that made men seem equals. That democratic spirit, John told Abby, was "very disagreeable to many gentlemen in the colonies."

John grew impatient at the slow pace of the proceedings. Rising early for breakfast, he read papers and pamphlets or wrote letters for an hour until the barber arrived. Reaching the Congress at nine, he engaged in debate until three.

"Then we adjourn, and go to dine with some of the nobles of Pennsylvania at four o'clock," he wrote Abby, "and feast upon ten thousand delicacies, and sit drinking Madeira, Claret and Burgundy, till six or seven, and then go home fatigued to death with business, company, and care. . . . Shall be killed with kindness in this place!" It vexed him that the Congress did not work nights instead. "Tedious indeed is our business, as slow as snails. I have not been used to such ways!"

He had accomplished little by the time the First Congress was ready to adjourn. About all radicals and conservatives could agree on was a tactful toast at social gatherings: "May the sword of the parent never be stained with the blood of her children."

When the Second Continental Congress opened in May 1775, John became convinced that the only way resistance could succeed was if the delegates were forced to recognize the Minutemen of Massachusetts as the nucleus of a Continental Army. To persuade them, he decided to nominate an eminent Virginian military man as their general.

"I am determined this morning," he told Sam in June, "to make a direct motion that Congress should adopt the army before Boston, and appoint Colonel Washington commander of it."

His ruse succeeded. "This appointment will have a great effect," he wrote Abby exultantly, "in securing the union of these colonies."

When Washington was given a great parade to honor his departure north, John felt pangs of envy and self-pity.

"Such is the pride and pomp of war," he wrote Abby glumly. "I, poor creature, worn out with scribbling for my bread and my liberty, low in spirits and weak in health, must leave others to wear the laurels which I have sown; others to eat the bread which I have earned; a common case."

Having created a national army, John now proposed building a navy as well, to attack British merchant ships. He agitated constantly for the manufacture of more and more gunpowder, which required saltpeter. "I am determined never to have saltpeter out of mind," he wrote James Warren, "but to insert some stroke or other about it in every letter for the future. It must be had!" He urged Abby to get her friends making it, and she did.

He irritated moderates in the Congress—"the Cool Considerate Men," he called them scornfully—by persistently proposing Independence. After twenty-three tries, he had still failed to get the subject debated.

The Second Congress settled down into a duel between the "conciliation men" and the "liberty men." The conciliators, now led by Pennsylvanian John Dickinson, insisted that the King was sending peace commissioners, and that it would be foolhardy for the Congress to take any rash action until the Crown had had a chance to offer a compromise.

John Adams scoffed at their hopes as "a bubble . . . as arrant an illusion as ever was hatched in the brain of an enthusiast, a politician or a maniac." During 1776 he forged to the front as leader of the radicals—ahead even of Sam, who was primarily interested in Massachusetts, while John was now obsessed with the dream of a Continental Government.

He emphasized his quarrelsome points by thumping on the floor with his hickory walking stick, and refused to be shut up. The conservatives grew increasingly furious at his passionate speeches, his impatience with disagreement, his absolute conviction that he alone was right.

Unable to win Independence at one fell swoop, John tried to sneak it in a piece at a time. He persuaded colony after colony to imitate the example of Massachusetts by setting up an independent people's government. When South Carolina did so in March, John exulted, "If North Carolina and Virginia should follow South Carolina's example, it will spread through all the rest of the colonies like electric fire. We are advancing by slow but sure steps to that mighty Revolution."

His greatest resistance came from the middle colonies— New York, Pennsylvania, New Jersey, Maryland. The harder he pressed them, the more stubbornly they resisted John's pleas for unity in breaking away from England.

He grew testy when hot-blooded Sons of Liberty back home scolded him for being too slow in getting Congress to move. But he, too, was impatient for action and fed up with empty oratory. "Nothing was said today," he groaned. "Nothing is likely to be said tomorrow or the day after or the day after that, but what has already been repeated and hackneyed a hundred times before. All the gentlemen in the Congress want is delay, delay; thus only they hope to defeat us, and thus they will defeat us if they can."

John finally persuaded Congress to agree to recommend that all colonies set up their own independent governments. He wrote James Warren proudly, "This day the Congress has passed

the most important resolution that was ever taken in America."
Caesar Rodney wrote home, "Most of those here who are termed
the Cool Considerate Men think it amounts to a declaration of
Independence. It certainly savors of it."

Tories everywhere were dismayed, seeing John's resolution as
branding every Crown official an outlaw, and ending protection
for Americans supporting the King's cause.

Seated barechested in his stifling lodgings, John wrote the
news to Abby, boasting, "When I consider the great events
which are passed, and those greater which are rapidly advancing,
and that I may have been instrumental. . . . I feel an awe upon
my mind which is not easily described."

Now both Virginia and North Carolina instructed
their delegates at the Congress to vote for separation from
England. John wrote gleefully, "Every post and every day rolls
Independence in upon us like a torrent!"

Then on June 7th Richard Henry Lee rose for Virginia to
propose what the delegates would not endure listening to a
twenty-fourth time from that irritating, unshakable gadfly John
Adams—Independence as a new nation.

But even if they couldn't stand John, Dr. Benjamin Rush
noted, "Every member of Congress in 1776 acknowledged him
to be the first man in the House." So maybe the unpopular
cranky Yankee patriot who held such a high opinion of himself
was right, after all.

FOUR

"I Think I Am Very Brave":
Abigail Adams

Tactless John Adams fell in love with a girl who was the soul of tact. He courted Abigail Smith for two years while her mother kept delaying their marriage. Mrs. Smith, who came from a prominent Quincy family, considered John too rude, too brusque, too short, too plump, and too poor for Abby.

John finally lost his temper and exploded at his sweetheart's mother. She had absolutely no right, he shouted, to delay their wedding another day. Mrs. Smith gasped at this uncivil behavior. Wrathful sweetheart and outraged mother glared at each other. It was a major domestic crisis for Abby.

She tactfully put a finger over John's lips playfully, then kissed her mother on the cheek.

"Mama dearest," she purred with an irresistible smile, "have I not the promise of a noisy husband? Can he not roar like a very lion for the love of me?"

Her shrewd sauciness compelled the antagonists to smile, however wanly. Gaining control of himself, John had the sense to apologize and the storm blew over. Soon afterwards Mrs. Smith yielded to her persuasive daughter, and the wedding was held.

It took a special girl like Abby to love a social porcupine like John. Yet even the tactful Abby found it difficult to discuss things with her intense, dogmatic husband. "I can be more free with you in letters, John," she once wrote him, "than when we are together." He, on the other hand, did not hesitate to criticize her for poor posture, standing pigeon-toed, playing cards badly, and—when she vexed him by proving smarter—for "reading, writing and thinking too much."

What Abby thought about a great deal made her an early Women's Lib pioneer. Agreeing with John that Americans must be liberated from royal oppression, she also insisted that it was equally important to free women from male subjugation.

When John was at the Continental Congress working for a new Republic, Abby reminded him that its new code of laws should forbid husbands unlimited power over wives, because men were inclined to be tyrants if they could. Besides, why should women obey laws they had no voice or representation in framing? Wasn't that, in fact, why the colonies were fighting England?

"And not withstanding all your wise laws," Abby warned him tartly, ". . . we have it in our power, not only to free ourselves, but to subdue our masters, and without violence throw both your natural and legal authority at our feet."

A wife, in other words, could make life miserable for a tyrannical husband. But such was not the case with John and Abby Adams. No couple was ever more devoted to each other.

Abby was born on November 11, 1744, in the village of Weymouth, Massachusetts, daughter of a Congregational minister. Her health too delicate to let her attend school, she was educated largely by her doting grandparents, the Quincys, who had a vast private library. Their mansion was constantly filled with brilliant company, and much of the shrewd wit she heard during her summers there rubbed off on little Abby.

At ten she fell in love with sheep when her father gave her a lamb for a pet. Nursing sick ewes in his flock, she also enjoyed helping him at lambing time. But as she grew older, Abby was forced by her mother, who also criticized her for reading so many books, to leave all such "unfeminine" barn matters up to men. What on earth did a girl need with Shakespeare, Milton, and John Locke, when there was so much to be learned in useful arts like sewing, baking, housekeeping?

Brown-haired Abby was seventeen when twenty-six-year-old John Adams began calling at the Smith parsonage to discuss law with her father. He became increasingly aware of the quiet, thoughtful girl who sewed or read quietly in a candlelit corner of the parlor. One evening he teased her about the great books she studied so seriously. Abby resented his patronizing air.

Girls, she replied coldly, could be just as intellectually curious as young men. Intrigued, on his next visit John apologized for giving offense, and made amends by giving her one of his favorite books. Abby's clear brown eyes held his as she thanked him. When she vanished upstairs, a dazed John suddenly realized that he was in love and wanted nothing more in the world than to be Abigail Smith's husband.

It now seemed to him that she was a great beauty, although a more accurate description of Abby would find her pleasant-faced and charming. The first opportunity he had to be alone with her, he kissed her. To his joy Abby responded with a happy sigh. When they decided to become engaged, Pastor Smith—but not his wife—gave wholehearted approval.

During the two years of their engagement, John sometimes frightened Abby by his headstrong vehemence, but she soon learned how to cope with his moods. He told her gratefully, "You are teaching me kindness, dear Abby."

When they were forced to be apart, they wrote each other long love letters. "My soul and body have been thrown into disorder by your absence," he wrote her once.

"I think I write to you every day," Abby replied. "Shall I not make my letters very cheap? Don't you light your pipe with them? I care not if you do. 'Tis a pleasure to me to write. Yet I wonder I write to you with so little restraint, for as a critic I fear you . . . the only character in which I ever did or will fear you. . . . Don't you think me a courageous being? Courage is a laudable, a glorious virtue in your sex, why not in mine?"

She and John began married life in a little house in Braintree. His struggle to establish himself as a lawyer kept him away from home a good deal. Self-reliant Abby managed their small farm and growing family—five children in all—with cool efficiency. She never wasted a moment, too Puritan even to read except to improve her mind.

Abby thoroughly approved of her husband's struggle against Crown injustice and, indeed, sometimes even suggested that he was too cautious in his advice to Bostonians. Eyes flashing, she condemned the cowardice of preachers who urged submission to the will of the King.

When John's business began taking him into Boston almost daily, they moved to the city for several winters to spare him a freezing ten-mile ride back and forth from Braintree. He shoehorned their growing family into a tiny rented house near the waterfront. Abby never grew used to the smell of fish and tarred rope, nor to the sailors who stared in her windows. And when curfew rang, she had to bolt all the doors.

She grew even more homesick for Braintree when British troops landed in October 1768. Each dawn she woke up to the harsh sounds of drum and fife, marching feet, musket butts crashing on the cobblestones. She never uttered a word of complaint. John was content, and they were together.

But one day he told her glumly that she and the children would be seeing less of him, because he had been elected to the colony's House of Representatives, which now met in Cambridge. Moreover, he would have to give up most of his law practice for the meager pay of a legislator.

"Forgive me," he said miserably. "I have condemned you and the children to a life of uncomfortable poverty."

Abby wept, not for grief, but for pride. Taking his hands tenderly, she told him that she wanted only to share whatever life brought him, and feared nothing but separation. He had done the right thing, she said, to obey the call of the people.

Tragedy struck in February 1770 when their firstborn child died. Abby turned unnaturally quiet and listless, often sitting in the dark and staring out the window. A month later she was startled and frightened by an uproar and shots close to their house . . . the Boston Massacre. She was further upset when all of Boston turned against her husband for undertaking to defend the soldiers involved.

Shaking off her grief, Abby gave John the support and encouragement he badly needed from her. Restored to the comfort of her bright spirits, he no longer felt lost and lonely.

As tension mounted in Boston, Abby felt torn between her fear of violence and her love of liberty.

After General Gage had been made Governor, and British troops occupied Boston, she wrote her friend Mercy Warren, "The great anxiety I feel for my country, for you, and for our family renders the day tedious and the night unpleasant. . . . Did ever any kingdom or state regain its liberty, when once it was invaded, without bloodshed? I cannot think of it without horror."

She was frightened for John when he was elected a delegate to the First Continental Congress. What if Gage arrested him for treason, and he were tried and hanged in England?

"If you were dead, my dearest," she told him with deep emotion, "I would not wish to live an hour longer."

"You must not think such thoughts, Abby," he reproached her. "If I no longer needed you, the children would."

When the time came for his departure, she choked back her fears and tears so that John could leave for Philadelphia without being upset. As the coach rolled off with the delegates, right in front of British troops, a woman in the crowd seeing them off asked Abby if she was not proud of her brave husband. Abby nodded gravely, but could not speak.

Then she took the children home to Braintree.

Each day she wrote him what news she could gather about the colony's affairs, and how people felt about what was going on in Boston, Braintree and elsewhere. "The Governor," she wrote him in September 1774, "is making all kinds of warlike preparations. . . . The people are much alarmed."

Knowing how much John missed the children, Abby coached seven-year-old John Quincy to write his first letter. The future sixth President wrote the future second President, "I have been trying ever since you went away to learn to write you a letter. . . . I hope I grow a better boy, and that you will have no occasion to be ashamed of me when you return. . . . We all long to see you." One suspects that little John Quincy had more than a little aid in composing his scholarly note.

Abby fed the fires of John's impatience with the Congress. "The people in the country begin to be very anxious," she wrote him in October, "for the Congress to rise. . . . Their blood boils with indignation at the hostile preparations they are constant witnesses of."

She pressed him to do what he could to have slavery outlawed in the colonies, in order to stand with clean hands before the world. How, otherwise, could Americans claim to be fighting, she asked, "for what we are daily robbing . . . from those who have as good a right to freedom as we have"?

There was a joyful reunion when John returned home in November, thrilling her with a pretty blue cloak he had bought her. The days passed all too swiftly until it was time for him to leave for the Second Continental Congress.

The countryside was agitated with rumors of British troops leaving Boston to attack the towns. Abby told John that their house was becoming an inn for mustered militiamen seeking lodging and meals. "Sometimes," she added, "refugees from Boston, tired and fatigued, seek an asylum for a day, a night, a week. You can hardly imagine how we live. . . . I wish you were nearer to us; we know not what a day will bring forth, nor what distress one hour may throw us into."

John replied anxiously, "In case of real danger . . . fly to the woods with our children."

He did not hesitate to suggest, meanwhile, that she gather military information for him. In June he wrote, "Let me know what guards are kept, and who were principally concerned in the battle at Grape Island, as well as that at Chelsea."

Abby's patriotic fervor rose with increasing danger, overriding her earlier fears. "Necessity," she wrote John, "will oblige Gage to take some desperate steps. . . . We live in continual expectations of alarms. Courage I know we have in abundance; conduct I hope we shall not want; but powder—where shall we get a sufficient supply?"

In the same letter she begged John to send her something she characterized as of the highest importance to her—a bundle of pins. "The cry for pins is so great," she explained, "that what I used to buy for seven shillings . . . are now twenty shillings, and not to be had for that."

On June 17th the roar of guns woke her at dawn. Messengers stopping for water at her farmhouse told her that a battle was raging on Bunker Hill. Abby ran to a nearby hill and watched with stunned eyes as British warships pounded Charlestown, burning it to ashes. Weeping, she wondered now many friends she knew lay dead in its smoking ruins.

"How many have fallen, we know not," she wrote John that night. "The constant roar of the cannon is so distressing that we cannot eat, drink or sleep."

She grew indignant at John's reports of his inability to force the Congress to break with England.

"Does every member feel for us?" she wrote passionately. "Can they realize what we suffer? And can they believe with what patience and fortitude we endure the conflict? Nor do we even tremble at the frowns of power."

She told him that she had decided to safeguard his valuable law library by moving it to his brother's place, because British troops from New York were reported headed toward Braintree. "But we have got to that pass," she added defiantly, "that a whole legion of them would not intimidate us. I think I am very brave, upon the whole. If danger comes near my dwelling, I suppose I shall shudder. We want powder, but with the blessing of Heaven, we fear them not."

John replied, "You ask, Can they realize what we suffer? I answer, No. They can't. They don't. . . . You sustain with so much fortitude the shocks and terrors of the times. You are really brave, my dear. You are a heroine." As her reward he was sending her "two great heaps" of her precious pins.

She thanked him profusely, sighing, "You can hardly imagine how much we want many common small articles. . . . I endeavor to live in the most frugal manner possible, but I am many times distressed." Could dear John also manage to send her a pound of pepper and two yards of Belgian woolens?

In July she reported, "The present state of the inhabitants of Boston is that of the most abject slaves, under the most cruel and despotic of tyrants." People were being arrested for wiping their faces with white handkerchiefs because of British suspicions that this was a "signal of mutiny." Householders were warned to keep off rooftops, or face execution for observing British military movements.

"Inhabitants dare not to look out of their houses," she wrote John, "nor to be heard or seen to ask a question." She was outraged at British treatment of homes they occupied, reporting the misery of a lady whose house was requisitioned by General John Burgoyne: "She saw raw meat cut and hacked upon her mahogany tables, and her superb damask curtains and cushions exposed to the rain as if they were of no value."

Although the letters she and John exchanged were full of the crisis, Abby at times complained that he was so preoccupied with the American cause as to sound more politician than husband. "I want some sentimental effusions of the heart," she complained once. "I am sure you are not destitute of them. Or are they all absorbed in the great public? . . . Being part of the public, I lay claim to a larger share than I have had."

An epidemic of war diseases swept Massachusetts. Among those who died were Abby's mother, John's brother Elihu and Abby's servant. She and the children all caught a disease but recovered. " 'Tis a dreadful time with the whole province," she wrote John. "Sickness and death are in almost every family.

I have no more shocking and terrible idea of any distemper, except the plague, than this."

Separation began to wear heavily on them both. "In the twelve years we have been married," she wrote John ruefully in October, "I believe we have not lived together more than six." He replied, "Oh, if I could only annihilate time and space!" If only Abby could come to Philadelphia with the children, he would be "proud and happy as a bridegroom."

But they were not wealthy like John Hancock and his Dolly. Abby knew that he needed her to look after their farm, cattle, and property, and to raise food for their large family. Prices had skyrocketed and their savings had dwindled.

Fretting that he might not be able to afford to send their children to Latin School and Harvard, John wrote Abby guiltily, "I will not bear the reproaches of my children—I will tell them that I . . . labored to procure a free Government for them . . . and if they do not prefer this to ample fortune, to ease and elegance, they are not my children, and I care not what becomes of them."

In addition to all else she did, Abby had to be her children's teacher as well, because the schools were closed. She dutifully heeded John's reminder:

"John Quincy has genius, and so has Charles. Take care that they don't go astray. Cultivate their minds, inspire their little hearts."

It was a lonely life for her, despite occasional visits from patriot leaders like Benjamin Franklin, whom she found "social but not talkative, and, when he spoke, something useful dropped from his tongue." He invited her to Philadelphia.

"I shall wish to be there, unless you return," Abby wrote John. "I have been like a nun in a cloister, ever since you went away. . . . My evenings are lonesome and melancholy."

By May of 1776 she was as impatient as John himself to have Congress declare Independence. To spur him on she wrote, "A people may let a king fall, yet still remain a people; but if a king let his people slip from him, he is no longer a king. And as this is most certainly our case, why not proclaim [it] to the world . . . ? Shall we not be despised by foreign powers for hesitating so long at a word?"

"I think you shine as a stateswoman . . . as well as a farmeress," he replied admiringly. "Pray where do you get your maxims of state? They are very apropos."

In the midst of this struggle he was disconcerted when the people of Massachusetts elected him Chief Justice.

"What shall I do with my office?" he wrote Abby. "I want to resign for a thousand reasons. Would you advise me?"

"If I was to consult only my own private satisfaction and pressure," she replied, "I should request you to resign it; but alas . . . I think you qualified and know you disposed to serve your country. I must advise you to hold it. . . . And in saying this I make a sacrifice."

John wrote back gratefully, "Your sentiments of the duties we owe to our country are such as become the best of women. . . . Among all the disappointments and perplexities which have fallen to my share in life, nothing has contributed so much to support my mind as the choice blessing of a wife whose capacity enabled her to comprehend, and whose pure virtue obliged her to approve, the views of her husband. . . . I read and read again your charming letters, and they serve me, in some faint degree, as a substitute for . . . the writer."

Despite his longing sighs for her in almost every letter, she knew that she could not afford to join him in Philadelphia like the wives of some richer delegates. On June 3, 1776, four days before Richard Henry Lee rose to propose Independence, she wrote John why it was impossible for her to come:

"It is my duty to attend with frugality and economy to our own private affairs. . . . Here I can serve my partner, my family, and myself, and enjoy the satisfaction of your serving your country."

FIVE

The Thunder Master:
Benjamin Franklin

If Benjamin Franklin's head was filled with all kinds of amazing ideas, his feet were firmly planted on the ground. He was a genius because he was at one and the same time a great visionary—yet as practical as a spoon.

In one of his numerous ocean crossings he was almost shipwrecked on a rocky coast. He demonstrated his practicality by writing his wife Deborah, "Were I a Roman Catholic perhaps I would build a chapel to some saint, but as I am not if I were to vow at all it would be to build a lighthouse."

On another occasion as he witnessed the first trial balloon flight, a spectator next to him grunted, "What good is it?" Benjamin indicated the breadth of his vision by replying dryly, "What good is a newborn baby?"

Franklin was born January 17, 1706, in a little frame house in Boston, the youngest son of ten children born by his father's second wife. His father was a soap- and candle-maker.

As a boy Benjamin was plump and sturdily built, with bright eyes indicating a superior intelligence. When he was seven, he paid another boy a pocketful of Christmas gift pennies for a cheap whistle. He enjoyed tooting it until his brothers and sisters taunted him for paying four times its value.

"I cried with vexation," he recalled, "and the reflection gave me more chagrin than the whistle gave me pleasure."

Thereafter he exercised great thrift, explaining, "When I was tempted to buy some unnecessary thing, I said to myself, 'Don't give too much for the whistle,' and I saved my money."

Because his father could not afford much education for his large family, Benjamin went to work in the tallow shop at the age of ten. But he made up for his lack of formal schooling by borrowing and reading books, often overnight, teaching himself geometry, science, grammar, history, and literature.

While cutting wicks, dipping candle molds and running errands, his fertile mind teemed with imaginative ideas. At twelve he made broad paddles for his hands and feet to give him greater swimming power. Then he made himself into a sailboat by building a large paper kite, holding it aloft while floating and letting the wind pull him across the pond.

His father apprenticed him to his half-brother James, who had a printing office. Benjamin persuaded James to pay him what his board cost and let him board himself. Turning vegetarian, Benjamin was able to buy books with the savings. When James began publishing *The New England Courant,* Benjamin wanted to write for it but knew he would only be laughed at as a kid brother.

So, writing humorous articles signed "Mrs. Silence Dogood," he slipped them under the office door at night. James was impressed and published them. Their sly wit and shrewd common sense won high praise from readers. But when "Mrs. Dogood" poked fun at the Governor, James was arrested for it. Alarmed, Benjamin confessed that he was the real culprit and apologized to the Governor's Council. James was released.

Far from being grateful, his brother gave him a thrashing for getting him into trouble. Benjamin indignantly ran away, boarding a sloop bound for New York.

He arrived in Philadelphia in October 1723 with only one Dutch dollar, the shirts and stockings stuffed in his pockets his only luggage. Stopping at a bakery, he paid a few pennies for three enormous rolls, put one under each arm and chewed hungrily on the third as he searched for work.

He found a job in a print shop, where his cheerful, witty personality quickly made him many friends. By the age of twenty-four, Benjamin owned his own printing business and was publisher of the *Pennsylvania Gazette.* "I dressed plainly," he wrote. "I was seen at no places of idle diversion. I never went out a-fishing or shooting . . . and to show that I was not above my business, I sometimes brought home the paper I purchased at the stores through the streets in a wheelbarrow."

In 1730 he married his landlady's daughter, Deborah Read. She was already married to a man who had deserted her, so theirs was a common-law union. To make their arrangement even more unique, Deborah adopted an out-of-wedlock son Benjamin had acquired, William, who later became royal Governor of New Jersey. Benjamin and Deborah had two children, one of whom died.

Semi-illiterate and incapable of sharing Benjamin's encyclopedic interests, Deborah was nevertheless devoted to the husband she called "Pappy." Although he became something of a ladies' man, enormously fussed over by women as he became famous, Benjamin never ceased being fond of his wife.

"It was lucky for me that I had one as much disposed to industry as myself," he wrote of her. "She assisted me cheerfully in business, folding and stitching pamphlets, tending shop, purchasing old linen rags for the paper makers, etc. We kept no idle servants, our table was plain and simple, our furniture of the cheapest."

His business thrived, never more so than in 1732 when he began publishing *Poor Richard's Almanack,* which he continued for twenty-five years. It was read by ordinary citizens who hardly read anything else, because it was full of useful information as well as the scraps of wit and wisdom of Benjamin Franklin, which he attributed to his alter ego, "Poor Richard."

By age forty-two, he was economically secure enough to retire from business and devote the rest of his life to "philosophical studies and amusements," in between dedicated services for the public good.

As the spark plug of a discussion club, he led its members in bringing about all kinds of civic improvements to Philadelphia—forming the first police force; paving and lighting the city's streets; starting the first circulating library in America; organizing the city's first hospital; setting up an academy that became the University of Pennsylvania.

A man of incredible energy and endless curiosity, in 1742 he invented something more warming and less wasteful than a fireplace—the Franklin stove, which transformed the heating systems of the nation. Not bothering to patent it, he never made a dime out of it. No sooner had he solved one scientific problem than he lost interest in it and was off eagerly experimenting with another.

His inventions included bifocal glasses; an improved anchor for ships; a combination chair-table such as schoolrooms use; an armchair with a foot pedal that rocked it and waved a large fan to keep off flies.

A keen observer of nature, Benjamin was constantly driven to discover the "why" of things. By experimenting with color cloths on snow, he found that black absorbed heat and white reflected it, which led him to recommend wearing white clothes in the tropics. Observing the moisture sneezed by people with colds, he deduced that cold-germs were introduced into the air in this manner, and insisted upon sleeping with his bedroom windows open to keep fresh air circulating.

The phenomenon of electricity fascinated him. Experiments to prove that lightning was sky-made electricity led him to invent and name the first battery. To demonstrate its use, he sought to kill a turkey for dinner by electric shock, then to roast it electrically. Unfortunately getting in the way of the current, he received a nasty shock.

Recovering, he observed dryly, "Well, I meant to kill a turkey—and instead I nearly killed a goose!"

In 1752, going out with his son William in a violent storm, he raised a kite with a metal key on the ground end of the string. When wet kite and string were swept up into a black thunder-cloud, they charged the key with electricity that Benjamin stored in a Leyden jar. His agile mind immediately sought to put his discovery to practical use.

The result was the lightning rod to attract storm bolts to a high metal post, then lead them harmlessly into the ground—an invention used today all over the world to protect buildings from being hit and set on fire by lightning.

As a result of his public posts and civic activities, he grew increasingly involved in political affairs. In 1751 when Britain sent a shipment of prisoners and slaves to the colonies to be rid of both, Benjamin suggested dryly that the colonies reciprocate Parliament's kindness by sending back a gift of American rattlesnakes. Nevertheless his prestige was so great that the Crown appointed him deputy postmaster general for the colonies in 1753.

The Pennsylvania Assembly sent Benjamin to England in 1757 to represent the colony's interests. Even though London society lionized him as America's most brilliant thinker, he preferred to live modestly as a lodger in the home of widow Margaret Stevenson and her daughter Polly, who quite spoiled him with their care and catering.

When it became clear that he would be staying abroad a long time, Benjamin urged Deborah to join him, but she refused to leave Philadelphia or permit their daughter to do so. A plain, simple woman, Deborah was sometimes embarrassingly loud and anything but genteel. She knew that she would feel out of place in the sophisticated society of the lords and ladies of her husband's world. Benjamin knew it too, and did not press her.

"Old trees cannot be transplanted," he sighed.

Benjamin was soon acting as agent not only for Pennsylvania, but also for New Jersey, Georgia, and Massachusetts. Enormously popular as a diplomat, he grew fond of the British in turn—*too* fond, Sam Adams worried. "Of all the enviable things England has," Benjamin had written home in 1763, "I envy it most its people."

Remembering his miraculous climb from a workbench making candle wicks to the castles and palaces of England as America's chief representative, Benjamin had to pinch himself to be sure he wasn't just dreaming. But he never let his prestige and acclaim go to his head, always recalling the advice of the eminent New England minister Dr. Cotton Mather, whose house he had visited as a young man of eighteen.

Dr. Mather cautioned him about the house's low beams, but as they moved about Benjamin forgot. The minister suddenly cried "Stoop! Stoop!" But it was too late and Benjamin cracked his head. "Ah, young man," sighed Dr. Mather, "if you will only remember to stoop before the beams of life, you will miss many hard thumps!" Benjamin wrote later, "I often think of that when I see pride mortified and misfortunes brought upon people by their carrying their heads too high."

In 1765 he sought to avoid a collision with the hard, immovable beams of the British palace after Parliament passed the Stamp Act against his protest. When Sam Adams raised a furor in the colonies, Benjamin wrote home urging his fellow Americans to pipe down and stop being so radical.

For the first time in his life Benjamin found himself unpopular at home. It began to be said that he had sold out to the Crown, seduced by the aristocrats he socialized with. Hotheads threatened to burn his Philadelphia home. Deborah sent their daughter to New Jersey for safety, but refused to budge herself. A brother and a nephew joined her with guns.

"We turned one room into a [powder] magazine," she wrote Benjamin. "I ordered some sort of defense upstairs, such as I could manage myself." But the danger passed when Benjamin redeemed himself by vigorous efforts to compel Parliament to repeal the hated Stamp Act. At a hearing in the House of Commons he was asked about the feelings Americans had entertained toward the British before the Act had been passed.

"The best in the world," Benjamin vowed. "They submitted willingly to the government of the Crown."

What would be the consequences if Parliament failed to repeal the Act? "A total loss of the respect and affection the people of America bear to this country, and of all the commerce that depends on that respect and affection."

His testimony greatly influenced the repeal of the Stamp Act, and his popularity at home soared once more.

Benjamin was shocked when Parliament replaced the Stamp Act with the Townshend taxes. He indignantly advised the colonies to band together in boycotting British goods until these taxes, too, were repealed. One King's minister upbraided him angrily for his "treachery" to King and country.

"While I have been thought here too much of an American," he replied with a sigh, "I have in America been deemed too much of an Englishman." But the British now began to intercept and read his mail, so Benjamin sent his letters home by private messenger. Convinced now that the Crown was too arrogant to compromise, he began to counsel open defiance.

In a last effort to patch up the quarrel between the Crown and the colonists, Benjamin offered to pay for the spilled tea in Boston Harbor out of his own pocket. Parliament would not hear of it, although some members hinted that their votes were for sale if the price was right. To encourage the anti-British boycott, Benjamin wrote home ironically:

"If America would save for three or four years the money she spends in fashions and fineries and fopperies of this country, she might buy the whole Parliament, Minister and all!"

One day the British ministry sent General Howe to see Benjamin secretly. Howe hinted that if Benjamin could persuade the colonists to end their opposition, he "might with reason expect any reward in the power of government to bestow." Benjamin coldly replied that his patriotism had no price tag. This attempt to bribe him, he wryly told his son, had all the elegance of "what the French vulgarly call 'spitting in the soup'!" He knew now that his usefulness in England was at an end.

His decision to return home was accelerated by the melancholy news in March 1775 that Deborah, his patient wife from whose side he had been absent for eighteen years, had died.

When he left England, the American whose formal schooling had ended at the age of ten took with him honorary degrees from Oxford and St. Andrews, to add to those already awarded him by Harvard and Yale.

He arrived home in May 1775, after the battles of Lexington and Concord had been fought. The Pennsylvania Assembly immediately chose him as a representative to the Second Continental Congress, where he worked openly for Independence.

Now sixty-nine, dressed in plain Quaker clothes, he often made his entrance into the Congressional chamber in a sedan chair carried by servants. Racked with gout, for which he wore a foot bandage, he sometimes could not stand long enough to make a speech. He then wrote it out and had it read for him.

"I was but a bad speaker," he admitted later, "never eloquent, subject to much hesitation in my choice of words, hardly correct in language, and yet I generally carried my points." Jefferson said he had never heard Benjamin speak for as much as ten minutes at a time. John Adams scornfully described Benjamin as he saw him—"from day to day, sitting in silence, a great part of the time asleep in his chair."

But when Benjamin did speak out, he was listened to carefully and his opinion carried great weight. If hot-tempered delegates threatened each other with their canes, he was always the peacemaker. They had all gathered together, he reminded them gently, "to consult, not to contend with each other."

The delegates compelled him to serve on ten committees, and made him postmaster general to set up a postal system "for the speedy and secure conveyance of Intelligence from one end of the continent to the other." The Crown had fired him as its deputy postmaster general, Benjamin said proudly, for refusing to be "corrupted by the office to betray the interests of my country."

In July 1775 Benjamin drew up and presented to the Congress the first concrete plan for a confederation of the colonies, to be called, "the United Colonies of North America." Jefferson supported it, but noted that the majority of delegates were "revolted" by it. "We found that it could not be passed," he wrote, because conservatives warned it would infuriate England and end all hopes of a peaceful settlement.

Fellow delegates nevertheless chose Benjamin to head a Committee of Secret Correspondence to create support for the American cause in Europe, where no man had a wider circle of influential friends—politicians, financiers, scientists, philosophers, publishers, writers, aristocrats. Benjamin's committee was the first American State Department.

In December 1775 a Frenchman named Achard de Bonvouloir called upon Benjamin to suggest that private deals could be arranged for the Americans to buy European munitions, paying with American products. He insisted that he was acting as an individual, but Benjamin correctly guessed that he was an agent for the court of France. King Louis XVI saw this arrangement as a way of weakening his enemy, England, without the risk of being accused of doing so officially. So Benjamin at once dispatched Silas Deane to France to negotiate arrangements.

As the battle between the radicals and the conservatives raged in the Congress, Benjamin used all his tact and diplomatic skill to calm the terrible-tempered John Adams and soothe his angry enemies, teaching both that there was more than one way to skin a cat and make a nation free.

SIX

The Rich Rebel:

John Hancock

Once, when John Hancock was serving sixty guests at dinner, a servant who was removing a huge, beautiful, imported cutglass centerpiece from the table let it slip. The tremendous crash silenced all conversation. In the awed hush that followed, John called out to the horrified servant, "James, break as many as you like, but please don't make such a confounded noise about it!"

He loved playing the role of delightful host to the popular leaders of the Massachusetts colony, and it tickled his vanity to be regarded as a wealthy patron of the people's cause who cared nothing for the cost or risk to his fortune. In actuality, John first joined the radicals because Parliament's taxes hurt his merchant trade badly, but Britain's use of force to collect them outraged him into becoming a champion of American freedom.

His greatest weakness was an incurable vanity. John Adams at least had the saving grace of knowing himself, admitting that he was "puffy, vain, conceited," and that vanity was his "cardinal folly." John Hancock, on the other hand, could write his fiancée boastfully of his entrance into Philadelphia for the Second Continental Congress, "the carriage of your humble servant, of course, being first in the procession. . . . In short, no person could possibly be more noted than myself."

Born in North Braintree on January 23, 1737, John was adopted at seven upon the death of his father, a minister, by a childless uncle, the richest merchant of Boston. He was brought up with every advantage money could buy.

The man who taught him to write his famous signature with a bold flourish was Master Holbrook of his Latin School, the most famous writing teacher in Boston, who taught an elegant "Boston style" of penmanship. Like all boys of that period, he was trained to begin all nouns with capital letters, because writing teachers considered that lots of capital letters on a page looked graceful.

Graduating from Harvard at seventeen, John was put to work assisting his uncle. For six years he mastered every detail of the shipping trade, and in 1760 was sent to England to learn the European end of the business.

A normal gay blade with a roving eye for the girls, John created gossip in London by wooing the housemaid of one of his uncle's agents and by the vanity of his dress.

When his uncle made him a partner in 1763, John was a handsome young Beau Brummel, cutting a fine figure in a coat of scarlet or blue lined with silk and embroidered with gold, his frilled white waistcoat and linen trimmed with lace cuffs, white silk stockings and gold-buckled shoes. Few save Sam Adams saw in this aristocratic peacock the potential for a dedicated revolutionary.

Thomas Hancock died in 1764, leaving his wharf, warehouse, ships, import business, and personal fortune to his nephew. At twenty-seven, John became the richest and most important entrepreneur in the colony of Massachusetts. But business was bad that year, and when Parliament passed the Sugar Act, John did not hesitate to dodge the tax by smuggling in his sugar cargoes.

Hearing that the Stamp Act would be passed next, he wrote to his agents in London, "It is very cruel. . . . These taxes will greatly affect us; our trade will be ruined . . . and in the end Great Britain must feel the effects of it."

Logically, John's great wealth and social prominence should have made him a Tory. But Sam Adams won him over to the radicals by shrewdly appealing to his desire to save his business, convincing John that the Sons of Liberty were the best hope of ending unjust and crippling taxes.

Crown officials were furious when the richest citizen of New England began to champion the radical cause. They considered the twenty-eight-year-old merchant worse than a traitor, calling him a fool because he had so much to lose by defying Parliament. But John was beginning to see the connection between taxation without consent and lack of freedom.

"I believe that not a man in England, in proportion to estate, pays the tax that I do," he wrote to his agents. "I will not be a slave. I have a right to the liberties and privileges of the English Constitution and I, as an Englishman, will enjoy them."

News of the repeal of the Stamp Act was brought to the colonies on John's brig *Harrison.* Boston went wild with delight. Church bells pealed, guns boomed, drums rolled, houses were lit up from cellar to attic. Outside John's big stone house opposite the Common, a platform was built for a great illumination of fireworks. John sent two hogsheads of wine out to the dancing crowds, while he celebrated privately with Sam Adams and other Sons of Liberty.

But when the Townshend Acts replaced the Stamp Act, an angry John began smuggling in every taxed article, and other merchants followed his lead. To stop them Parliament sent six new customs commissioners and a large staff of clerks, together with a frigate patrol. John vowed publicly that he would not permit any customs officer to board any of his cargo ships arriving from London.

In June 1768 his sloop *Liberty* docked at night with a taxable cargo of wine that the captain at once prepared to smuggle ashore. A customs inspector, however, managed to steal aboard to inventory the cargo. Informed, John rushed to the wharf with ten Sons of Liberty, and threw him off the sloop. It was the first act of physical opposition to Crown officers by respectable American citizens.

When the British sent General Gage with troops to occupy Boston, John indignantly told a town meeting, "Burn Boston and make John Hancock a beggar, if the public good requires it!" On the King's orders he was arrested and charged with smuggling. A conviction would mean the forfeit of all his wealth. But John Adams fought the case and won a dismissal of the charges for lack of evidence.

John Hancock was now hailed by his fellow citizens as a courageous hero who dared to risk his entire fortune in order to fight for a principle. His popularity made John vainer than ever. Turning temperamental, he refused to endure the slightest criticism from other radicals. When one suggested that he had much to learn as a leader, he sulked and threatened to resign from the cause.

John's appetite for glory made him secretly ambitious to snatch the leadership of the radical movement from Sam Adams. He felt that he would be a far more impressive and dignified leader. Sam privately distrusted John as a vacillating tycoon susceptible to flattery, but prized his financial aid, his influential name, and his devotion to the cause—as long as Sam had him under control.

Subtly guided by Sam, John led the struggle to unite all American merchants in a boycott of British goods—"nonimportation." He was dismayed when some greedy merchants welshed on their word, profiteering while John and those who stood by the pact suffered severe business losses. "In the matter of nonimportation," he wrote his London agents gloomily, "I . . . have been most fully, freely and cruelly used."

On the King's recommendation, Parliament rescinded the Townshend Acts, leaving only the tax on tea as a symbol of Crown authority. It was just this symbol, however, that John and the Sons of Liberty insisted upon resisting.

At least one million Americans drank tea twice daily. In Philadelphia, noted a British M. P., "the women are such slaves to it, that they would rather go without their dinners than without a dish of tea." John led a campaign to persuade them that tea drinking was both unpatriotic and unhealthy.

"Do not suffer yourself to sip the accursed stuff," his propaganda warned, "for if you do, the devil will immediately enter into you, and you will instantly become a traitor to your country." Tea tax collectors who fell afoul of Sam's mobs were seized, tarred, and feathered. Many had scalding tea poured down their throats as a "toast" to the King.

But with all other taxes removed, most Americans stopped paying attention to the radicals. As tensions eased, their ranks slimmed. John himself seemed to lose interest, winning public praise instead by building a bandstand on the Common to give Bostonians free concerts, presenting them with a fire engine, and arranging to light the city with street lamps.

When the tea ships arrived from England at the end of 1773, Hancock mounted a guard at the port to make sure the cargoes were not landed. At the town meeting in the Old South Church, he warned Bostonians, "The matter must be settled before midnight!" And when the crowd rushed out of the building toward the wharf, he shouted, "Let every man do what is right in his own eyes!"

One "Indian" at the Boston Tea Party later reported seeing John helping to dump a chest, claiming to recognize him "not only by his ruffles . . . but by his features . . . and by his voice, also, for he exchanged an Indian grunt and the expression, 'Me know you' . . . the password."

No attempt was made to prosecute either John Hancock or Sam Adams for their role in the Boston Tea Party, as it was felt hopeless to expect a Boston jury to indict them.

After Sam and John Adams left for the First Continental Congress in September 1774, the new Governor, General Gage, shut down the Massachusetts House of Representatives. Its members defiantly moved to Concord and organized the first Provincial Congress, electing John Hancock its President. He was also made chairman of a Committee of Safety, instructed to organize and equip a twelve thousand-man Minutemen militia.

But John was not too busy to fall in love. A colony gossip reported, "'Tis said John Hancock courts Dolly Quincy." Capricious Dorothy Quincy was a pretty girl with a high, intelligent forehead, dark, limpid eyes, well-defined nose, thin lips and attractive chin. She became his fiancée, but hectic events forced postponement of their marriage.

Defying Tory threats on his life, John continued open resistance to the Governor and the Crown. Some three hundred British officers in Boston concocted a plan to assassinate him and other radical leaders at a town meeting called in March 1775 to commemorate the Boston Massacre. Their plan was to hurl an egg at the first word spoken against the King, the signal for all to draw their swords and fall on the Sons of Liberty.

Ironically, according to a later account by a British colonel named James, the officer entrusted with the egg tripped and broke it in his hand, destroying the signal. When John began an anti-British speech, the officer shouted out instead, "Fie! Fie!" The crowd thought he was yelling "Fire!" and stampeded in panic for the nearest doors and windows.

Noting that John "and the rest of the villians" escaped without harm, Colonel James consoled himself with the reflection, "It would indeed have been a pity for them to have made their exits in that way, as I hope we shall have the pleasure before long of seeing them do it by the hands of the hangman."

King George sought to oblige by issuing orders to arrest both John Hancock and Sam Adams, and ship them to England to stand trial for treason. Warnings were sped to the radicals by British sympathizers, who were shocked by the King's stubborn determination to crush American protest forcibly.

To escape the British looking for them, John Hancock and Sam Adams were forced to hide out in Lexington at the home of the Reverend Jonas Clarke. John wrote Dolly, "I shall return as soon as possible, when I shall be with you; and, I hope, you will not be saucy." The flighty Dolly often behaved more like a prize still to be won than a fiancée. When it became clear that John could not return to Boston without risking his life, he begged her to visit him instead. Her aunt insisted she go, and chaperoned her to Lexington.

They were with him in April 1775 when patriot leader Joseph Warren sent Paul Revere to Lexington to warn John and Sam that Gage had British reconnaissance units searching the countryside for them, and to warn the Minutemen that Redcoats were coming to destroy the colony's munitions at Concord.

It was after midnight when Revere galloped up breathlessly to Reverend Clarke's house. As all within were asleep, a Minuteman guard told the midnight rider not to make so much noise. "Noise!" exploded Revere. "You'll have noise enough before long. The Regulars are coming out!"

Hearing the commotion, John stuck his head out the window and called, "Come in, Revere. We are not afraid of *you*!"

All in the house crowded around the messenger while he told them the news. John immediately vowed to pick up a gun and join the Minutemen of Lexington, who were already mustering to oppose the Redcoats. Sam Adams told him not to be foolish, but John was eager to cut a gallant figure before Dolly. Jealous of Sam's prominence, he hungered for a more dramatic role than merely chief financier of the Sons of Liberty.

Sam pointed out that such bravado would only play into the King's hands. Their deaths would be a severe blow to the Independence movement. Alive they might yet bring about a declaration of war against Britain as delegates to the Second Continental Congress, scheduled to open in a month.

John was reluctantly persuaded that it was his duty to escape. Dolly decided to return to her father in Boston.

"No, madam," John said firmly, "you shall not return as long as there is a British bayonet in Boston."

"I am not under your control yet, Mr. Hancock!" she replied icily. "I *shall* go to my father!" And she did.

John was determined that the Congress must not fail. He sought to keep peace between radicals and conservatives in order to hold them together in the American cause. His task was not made easier by the jealousies and suspicions that men of one colony held toward those of another.

If his mind was on the Congress, his heart was troubled by Dolly. "I am almost prevailed on to think that my letters to . . . you are not read, for I cannot obtain a reply," he complained ruefully. "I have asked a million questions, and not an answer to one. . . . really take it extremely unkind."

Fortunately for John's peace of mind, he did not know that the capricious Dolly was too busy flirting with another handsome, rich, ladies' man she had just met—Aaron Burr. But for the severe disapproval of Dolly's aunt, John might have lost his fiancée to the future traitor.

When John Adams rose to nominate a general for the new Continental Army, he began by praising the man he had in mind as a man of "independent fortune, great talents and excellent universal character who would command the approbation of all America." As he spoke, Hancock beamed with pleasure, confident that Adams was talking about him.

"But as I came to describe Washington for commander," John Adams wrote later, "I never remarked a more sudden and striking change of countenance. Mortification and resentment were expressed as forcibly as his face could exhibit them. Mr. Samuel Adams seconded the motion, and that did not soften the President's physiognomy at all."

John Hancock's only claim to military distinction had been as a parade ground colonel of the Boston Cadets, but he felt that his high social position, wealth, service in the Sons of Liberty and Presidency of the Congress entitled him to the honor of being named Commander-in-Chief. Grieved at both Adamses for having slighted him, he never forgave them.

Soon afterward John wrote to Washington seeking a place under him, even "if it be to take a firelock and join the ranks as a volunteer." But the Commander-in-Chief knew that John was of far greater value as President of the Congress than he would be as just another officer, and denied the chagrined patriot his chance to become a military hero.

When the sweltering Congress adjourned for five weeks in August, John finally managed to put a ring on Dolly Quincy's finger. Since a price was on his head in Boston, she met him in Connecticut for an elaborate wedding ceremony attended by celebrated guests. Their honeymoon was a jolting trip by coach back to Philadelphia, where Dolly remained at John's side while he continued to preside over the Congress.

By October 1775 John Hancock despaired of getting the delegates to act together as a confederacy, instead of as thirteen separate colonies. Each colony had its own ideas of the best way to remedy the troubles with England. New Jersey talked of making a separate peace treaty. Massachusetts threatened to declare itself independent.

From Cambridge, Washington complained, "Connecticut wants no Massachusetts man in their corps. Massachusetts thinks there is no necessity for Rhode Islanders to be introduced among them." Virginia and Carolina volunteers were outraged that free Negroes were allowed to serve in the same New England regiments, grumbling that white Yankees were bad enough.

In the winter of 1775 John dominated a debate over whether Congress should order Washington to attack the British in Boston. "Nearly all the property I have in the world is in houses and other real estate in the town of Boston," he declared, "but if the expulsion of the British Army from it—and the liberties of our country—require their being burned to ashes, issue the order for that purpose immediately!"

When the Congress did, he wrote to Washington, "May God crown your attempt with success. I most heartily wish it, though individually I may be the greatest sufferer."

In early 1776 he brought Indian chiefs to Philadelphia to keep their tribes neutral in the struggle. Offering them presents as bribes, he also sought to impress them with American power by letting them review battalions marching off to Boston. The Indians also decided to give John something to think about, as Caesar Rodney observed: "Twenty-one Indians of the Six Nations gave Congress a war dance yesterday."

Learning that General Howe planned to attack New York, John wrote to Washington urging him to come to Philadelphia for an immediate conference, and stating that the Hancocks would be honored to play host to the General and his lady. When the Washingtons arrived, however, they preferred to be guests of fellow Virginian Peyton Randolph. John's hurt vanity led him to nurse a grudge against Washington.

On June 7th there was a roar of excitement in the Congress when a silken-clad Virginian asked to speak. John rapped slowly for order, like the tolling of the great bell that would soon ring aloft Independence Hall. Then he gave Richard Henry Lee the floor to offer the brash proposal that John had risked his fortune and his neck to make possible.

SEVEN

The Silent Redhead:
Thomas Jefferson

He had never been outside of Virginia. At twenty-three, he decided to broaden his horizons by driving a horse and buggy to New York. On the first day out his horse bolted and almost killed Thomas before it could be brought under control. Next day he rode for two hours in a drenching storm until he could find a house for shelter. On the third day when a ford proved too steep, he was submerged waist-deep in water as one wheel went over a huge boulder, threatening to overturn the buggy.

In New York he met Elbridge Gerry, a Boston youth who ten years later would sign Jefferson's Declaration of Independence. Gerry asked whether his trip north had been exciting.

"Oh, yes!" Thomas replied. Then he showed Gerry his notes on flora and fauna he had seen, and different kinds of coins in circulation that he had collected en route.

John F. Kennedy once described a group of Nobel Prize winners he had invited to dine in the Executive Mansion as "the most extraordinary collection of talent . . . that has ever been gathered together at the White House—with the possible exception of when Thomas Jefferson dined alone."

An early biographer, James Parton, described Thomas in 1775 as "a gentleman of thirty-two who could calculate an eclipse, survey an estate, tie an artery, plan an edifice, try a cause, break a horse, dance a minuet and play the violin."

Thomas Jefferson was also a highly intelligent humanitarian who hated class distinctions, introduced the first American laws guaranteeing total religious freedom, and was an early fighter for universal education and emancipation. He was a quiet but warm man of enormous personal charm.

Thomas's father was a self-educated surveyor and planter who achieved social position by marrying into the distinguished Randolph family. The third of ten children, Thomas was born April 13, 1743, at Shadwell, the family home on a tobacco plantation. His father was a vigorous lover of the outdoors, noted for his fine mind and generous hospitality, which included entertaining many Indian friends.

Peter Jefferson taught his son how to ride, fish, paddle a canoe on the Rivanna, survive in the forest on game, and sleep in hollow trees for protection against wild beasts.

Red-haired Thomas grew up tall, lean, bronzed, strong, and self-reliant. He emulated his father's example of spending hours reading great books, often enjoying them as he floated down the Rivanna in the family canoe. His mother taught him social graces—singing, dancing, playing the violin.

Influenced by his father's view that the forest recognized no social distinctions, Thomas grew up with a distaste for arrogance and snobbery. He refused to copy the Virginians who behaved like British aristocrats, feeling that American conduct should reflect a democratic society. He even hated to be called "Mister" Jefferson, considering that plain "Thomas Jefferson" was enough. Despite his family's slaves, he considered slavery to be wrong, and opposed all special privileges.

He was fourteen when his father died. Although legally under the care of a guardian, he wrote later, "The whole care and direction of myself was thrown on myself entirely, without a relation or friend qualified to advise or guide me."

After an early education at a frontier school, he entered William and Mary College in Williamsburg at sixteen. Throwing himself into his studies, he pored over books as long as fifteen hours a day, keeping himself in good physical shape by running a mile out of town every evening. An insatiable curiosity led him to read everything that interested him, in addition to college studies.

"Three things became a passion with me," he said later. "Mathematics, music and architecture."

His chief relaxation was practicing on the violin. But there were other distractions. Despite its small size and lack of sidewalks or sewers, Williamsburg was the political, social, and cultural center of the upper South. During sessions of the legislature, rich planters flocked to the gay little town with their wives and daughters to mingle with the cleverest minds in Virginia. High fashion, horse racing, balls, brilliant receptions and dinners dominated the aristocratic scene.

Despite his democratic instincts and scholarly bent, Thomas found the social whirl exhilarating. Now a rawboned, broad-shouldered youth with red hair and freckles, he was not exactly handsome, but his pointed features were pleasant and illuminated by intelligence. A bit awkward because he stood well over six feet, and somewhat rustic because of his upbringing in the woods of western Virginia, he was nevertheless quite popular. Planters' daughters were charmed by his quizzical hazel eyes, soft voice, and bright conversation.

Enjoying gay company like any youth his age, Thomas made time to attend the races, join in card or dice games, and dance in the quadrilles, minuets, and Virginia reels at the Apollo Room of the Raleigh Tavern that livened things up for the young set. He even outfitted himself with a new flowered waistcoat, silk stockings, and laced hat.

Thomas's brilliant mind brought him to the attention of William Small, a Scottish mathematician and philosopher who had a tremendous influence upon him. When Small introduced him to Chancellor Wythe, they took him to their weekly dinners at the Governor's palace.

"At these dinners I have heard more good sense, more rational and philosophical conversations," Thomas wrote, "than in all my life besides." Taking along his fiddle, he often played chamber music with the Governor, a musician himself. Governor Fauquier sometimes invited the eighteen-year-old student to remain after the dinners for a game of cards.

Some of Thomas's fellow students, caught up in the excitement of cockfights, gambling, drinking, racing and running with tavern women, became wastrels. In later years Thomas marveled that, because of his youth, he had not followed a similar path. What had saved him, he felt, was the driving curiosity that kept him too busy pursuing intellectual activities that fascinated and challenged him.

"In a moment of temptation or difficulty," he recalled later, "I would ask myself, 'What would Dr. Small, Dr. Wythe, do in this situation?"

At nineteen he fell in love with seventeen-year-old Rebecca Burwell, nicknamed Belinda, a beautiful blonde belle with more admirers than she could handle. She let him have her portrait— "my dear picture," he called it—for his watch, but he was too sensitive and shy to put his adoration into words. He suffered jealous pangs as she used her flirtatious bright blue eyes to win flowery phrases from other admirers.

"Rebecca Burwell is the devil," he wrote unhappily in a notebook. "If not the devil, she's one of his imps."

Wanting to propose to her but dreading rejection, he grew tongue-tied whenever he tried. He could only, he lamented, speak "a few broken sentences, uttered in great disorder." To find the courage one night when he took her dancing at the Apollo Room, he drank too much. It did no good and next morning, suffering from a hangover, he wrote gloomily, "Last night, as merry as agreeable company and dancing with Belinda in the Apollo could make me, I never could have thought the succeeding sun would have seen me so wretched as I am now."

In January 1763, when Belinda had returned home, Thomas wrote to a friend, John Page, who lived near her, "How does R. B. do? Had I better stay here and do nothing, or go down and do less? . . . Inclination tells me to go, receive my sentence, and be no longer in suspense; but reason says, if you go, and your attempt proves unsuccessful, you will be ten times more wretched than ever." Like Miles Standish, he wanted his friend to propose for him.

Page refused, pointing out that if she did say no, well, there were plenty of other girls to marry. "No, no, Page," Thomas replied in despair. "If Belinda will not accept of my services, they will never be offered to another."

When his watch got wet, ruining her picture, he wrote Page, "Although it may be defaced, there is so lovely an image imprinted on my mind that I shall think of her too often, I fear, for my peace of mind."

He was stunned when Page wrote that he had waited too long, and that his beloved Belinda was getting married. At first Thomas felt beyond consolation. He told Page he was going to throw everything up and go to Europe for two or three years. If he "could not be cured of love in that time," he sighed miserably, then he was doomed to yearn after her forever.

But youthful heartbreak is seldom fatal. The distinguished-looking country squire with red silky hair now began to notice that there was no shortage of pretty girls in the colony of Virginia. But prettiness alone, after Belinda, no longer seemed enough. He wrote his friend Fleming that he could "view the beauties of this world with the most philosophical indifference," and was now more interested in a girl's mind. One exasperated Williamsburg girl exclaimed that she "never knew anyone to ask so many questions as Thomas Jefferson!"

One day in 1765 Thomas was deeply stirred by hearing Patrick Henry make his famous "If this be treason" speech at a session of the Virginia House of Burgesses, during a debate over the Stamp Act. Thomas had known Henry for some time, considering him a charming and eloquent backwoodsman.

Thrilled by his oratory and reflecting on Henry's defiance of the King, Thomas reached the conclusion that "rebellion to tyrants is obedience to God." It was the beginning of his dedication to the ideals of the American Revolution. He was already convinced of the virtues of democracy.

Admitted to the bar when he was twenty-four, Thomas won attention by his handling of two cases that shocked conservative Virginians. One involved a white woman who had borne a mulatto child sixty-five years earlier, for which the law had sentenced her to slavery. She had since borne another child, who in turn had a son. Her slave owner now insisted that her grandson was also, under the original law, his legal slave.

Thomas challenged the claim, arguing that "under the law of nature, all men are born free"—a phrase he was soon to use again in a famous document. The shocked judge did not even wait to hear the other side, quickly passing judgment in favor of the slave owner.

The second case involved the right of a church parish to remove its clergyman for disorderly conduct—drunkenness, profanity, fighting, and moral offenses. The church hierarchy argued that religious matters could not be decided by a civil court. Jefferson cited English precedents to prove that the civil authority was supreme, and won the case. His victory outraged those who held the church above the law.

Despite being controversial, his growing reputation led to his election to the Virginia House of Burgesses in 1769. The twenty-six-year-old legislator became highly regarded by his colleagues as a brilliant thinker and writer. But he was no orator like Patrick Henry, because his voice was too weak. He preferred, moreover, to read and reflect than make speeches.

Like Sam Adams, he was far less interested in money than in serving his fellow citizens. He resolved "never to engage, while in public office, in any kind of enterprise for the improvement of my fortune." Nor would he seek popularity at the expense of his principles. Hating slavery, he proposed a bill that would allow those slave owners who wished to do so to emancipate their slaves. Even this first mild step toward emancipation offended planters, who crushed the bill.

While the House of Burgesses was in session, Thomas frequently called at the mansion of John Wayles, a rich and successful lawyer, to discuss legislation. But he soon began calling for a different reason—Wayles's twenty-two-year-old widowed daughter, Martha Wayles Skelton.

She was a small, slender beauty with large hazel eyes and a mass of auburn hair that glinted in the sun. Cheerful and intelligent, she was a delightful companion, talented on both harpsichord and pianoforte. He began courting her with the same quiet, earnest determination he showed in winning court cases. "In every scheme of happiness she is . . . the principal figure," he soon confided to a friend. "Take that away, and it is no picture for me."

There were plenty of other suitors. One night two of them showed up simultaneously, clutching flowers and glaring at each other in the hall. Then they heard her playing the harpsichord and singing—she had an "uncommon singing voice," Thomas said. But there was also another sound—the joyful scraping of a violin. Then the latecomers noticed Thomas Jefferson's cloak hanging on the wall. Staring at each other disconsolately, they took their leave. It was just as well. Martha had already made up her mind to marry the handsome redhead with whom she made such beautiful music.

Determined that she would marry him, he had already thrown himself into building a house of his own design for them on top of Monticello. He had only partially completed it when the family homestead at Shadwell burned down.

"Your books were all lost in the fire," a slave told him, then added brightly, "but we saved your fiddle!"

Moving into his unfinished home with his mother and two sisters, Thomas wrote a friend gloomily that the lost books had cost two hundred pounds, but "would to God it had been the money, then it would never have cost me a sigh." It took him two years, and a quarter of his income, to rebuild a library with books ordered from London.

With less to read on hand, when he wasn't courting Martha he spent his time inventing things. Thomas's mind, like Franklin's, was too agile to keep focusing on any one subject for long. He created clocks that told the day as well as the hour, folding ladders, a dumb-waiter to bring wines up from cellar to fire-place, swivel chairs, and hanging beds.

When Martha finally said yes to him, Thomas joyfully sent to London for an engagement gift for her—a new pianoforte. He urged the agent to be sure its quality was "worthy of the acceptance of a lady for whom I intend it."

They were married at her father's home on January 1, 1772, in the midst of a thick snowstorm. Thomas had decided that there could be no better place for a honeymoon than on the mountaintop of Monticello, even though the mansion was still largely unfurnished. When they left in his two-horse carriage, the storm grew so bad that at length the wheels would not turn.

Abandoning the carriage, the bridal couple continued on horseback, laughing at the thick flakes that filled their mouths. They were still eight miles from Monticello when the snow was almost two feet deep. Reaching the mansion late at night, they found the fires all out and the servants—who had given up expecting them—in bed.

Thomas refused to wake them up, and the honeymooners took up their quarters on the floor in an empty room. Kindling a fire, Thomas produced a bottle of wine to warm them up. Laughing louder and louder at their absurd honeymoon as the wine disappeared, they greeted the rising sun with a tipsy duet.

At peace in his personal life, Thomas turned his attention back to Virginia's affairs. A staunch supporter of the New England radicals in their struggle against the Crown, he helped organize the Virginia Committee of Correspondence. He, Patrick Henry, and Richard Henry Lee led other young radicals in winning leadership of the House of Burgesses. They passed a resolution condemning taxation without representation.

Governor John Dunmore curtly dissolved the House for opposing the Crown. Next day Thomas and twenty-seven angry legislators met in the Apollo Room of the Raleigh Tavern in a rump session. Denouncing the British military invasion of Boston, they declared that "an attack on any one colony should be considered as an attack on the whole." Then they called for a Continental Congress to meet, and set up a convention in Williamsburg to elect delegates to that Congress.

When the British announced a blockade of Boston harbor for June 1, 1774, Thomas called upon Virginians to make that date a day of fasting and prayer. It was a shrewd propaganda move, making Virginians feel that they were directly involved in what was happening in Massachusetts. "The people met generally with anxiety and alarm in their countenances," Thomas noted, "and the effect of the day throughout the whole colony was like a shock of electricity, arousing every man."

He was selected to draw up official instructions to be given to Virginia's delegates to the Congress, instructions that he saw as an opportunity to proclaim Americans' defiance of the King. Composing the paper at Monticello, he wrote that immigration of Americans' forebears to the colonies gave England "no more rights over us than Danish emigration to England had given Denmark authority over England."

"Can any one reason be assigned," he demanded, "why 160,000 electors in the island of Great Britain should give law to four million in the States of America, every individual of whom is equal to every individual of them?"

He attacked the rights of kings: "Kings are the servants, not the proprietors of the people." King George had "no right to land a single armed man upon our shores," especially not "to send large bodies of armed forces, not made up of the people here, nor raised by the authority of our laws."

Too ill to attend the Williamsburg Convention, Thomas sent a messenger with two copies of his paper. One went to chairman Peyton Randolph, the other to Patrick Henry, in the hope that the great orator would declaim it to the convention.

Henry ignored it because, Thomas guessed wryly, he "was too lazy to read it (for he was the laziest man in reading I ever knew)." Randolph was greatly impressed, and read it aloud to the deputies. Thomas's powerful command of language stirred great admiration, but many deputies feared that his paper, in his own comment, was "too bold for the present state of things." So Virginia's delegates to the Continental Congress were given a mild set of instructions instead.

In the spring of 1775 he was well enough to be made a delegate to the Second Continental Congress, in place of Peyton Randolph, who had been named president of the Virginia Assembly. He made the journey in ten days.

When he took his seat in the Congress on June 21, other delegates were intensely curious about the long-legged, slender giant with brick-red hair who had written the explosive *Summary View* paper. Surprised at his youth—at thirty-two, he was next to the youngest man in the Congress—they were impressed by his quiet manner. He made no speeches, listened intently when important debates were in progress, and opened a book when boring trivia was being wrangled about.

"During the whole time I sat with him in the Congress," John Adams recalled, "I never heard him utter three sentences together." But Thomas rose when some conservatives threatened to stop Washington's appointment as Commander-in-Chief of an "Army of the United Colonies" because, they insisted, this move signified open revolution against the Crown.

"We are making this appointment in the name of the King," Thomas pointed out dryly, "and thus we are not fighting a revolution, but merely resisting the tyranny of a ministerial army." Then he sat down.

But he would soon have far more to say on the subject after Richard Henry Lee rose, on instructions from the Virginia Assembly, to move for immediate Independence.

EIGHT

The Disgusted General:
George Washington

The Father of his country was a most reluctant parent indeed. Even after the battle of Bunker Hill, every night at his New England headquarters he rose in the officers' mess to toast the King. Independence, George Washington said firmly, was not desired "by any thinking man in all North America."

Far from taking pride in his role as Commander-in-Chief of the Continental Army, he wrote his aide-de-camp, Joseph Reed, "Could I have foreseen what I have, and am likely to experience, no consideration upon earth should have induced me to accept this command. . . . We are told that we shall soon get the army completed, but I have been told so many things which have never come to pass, that I distrust every thing."

Nor was he overly fond of the Americans he was called upon to lead in battle. In August 1775 he wrote his cousin Lund Washington from Cambridge, "I daresay the men would fight very well (if properly officered) although they are an exceedingly dirty and nasty people."

The miracle of George Washington is that he was on the side of the American radicals at all. One of the richest men in Virginia, a slave-holding aristocrat who dressed in the finest of fashion and most elegant of uniforms, calm and conservative in temperament, he properly belonged in the ranks of those John Adams derisively called the Cool Considerate Men.

But Britain's violation of colonial rights offended his dignity as a Virginian, and in the end he proved more American patriot than British gentleman. When he did come over completely to the radical position of Independence as well as resistance, despite gloomy forebodings of disaster, no man fought for it more doggedly, intelligently, or courageously.

He was born at Bridges Creek, Virginia, on February 22, 1732. Contrary to popular opinion, he wasn't born with a silver spoon in his mouth. His father Augustin was a land-poor planter with a small four-room house on the Rappahannock in which George lived until he was fifteen.

His mother Mary Ball Washington was the second wife of his father, and by all accounts a tyrant of a woman. George's half-brother Lawrence said he was "ten times more afraid" of her than of their father, terming her in awe a "majestic woman."

Argumentative and illiterate, she constantly resented George's career as he pursued it because she felt that it led him to neglect her.

At ease only when out from under her domination, young George escaped as often as he could by visiting friends and relatives. A strong, muscular boy who loved to climb mountains and wrestle, he enjoyed challenges to his physical endurance, despite—or perhaps because of—frequent bouts of illness.

His father died when he was eleven, and George was left under the guardianship of Lawrence. Three years later, tired of school and eager to master a man's work, he asked Lawrence to persuade their mother to send him to England to study surveying. But Mary Washington flatly refused, nor would she permit George to join the British Navy. Lawrence argued.

"George is *my* son," she shrilled, "not yours!"

George persuaded a local surveyor to take him along as an apprentice to help mark boundary lines for new settlers in the wilderness. Enthusiastically tramping in mud, climbing mountains, and wading creeks in the most bitter weather, he learned enough by sixteen to become assistant to the official surveyor for Prince William County.

In and out of the wilderness for two years, George learned to be resourceful and stoical in the face of adversity, two qualities that would serve him well in the Revolution. But swamps infested with malaria-carrying mosquitoes gave him recurrent fevers, called "ague," throughout his life.

Although later portraits show him with a smooth skin, his face was actually pitted by smallpox he caught at nineteen when he accompanied Lawrence to Barbados because of his half-brother's poor health. It was the first and only time George was ever outside the borders of his country.

When Lawrence died of tuberculosis in 1752, George became manager of the family estate and plantations at Mount Vernon. He was now a young giant who wore a size thirteen shoe and stood over six feet four. "His movements and gestures are graceful," noted Captain George Mercer, "his walk majestic, and he is a splendid horseman."

His favorite relaxations were outdoor sports, especially hunting and fishing, and raising fine riding horses. He also socialized in the taverns with friends, his gray-blue eyes riveted on others as he talked or listened to politics.

When trouble with France threatened, he joined the Virginia militia and was made a major at nineteen. It was a curious trait of his that he never said no when asked to undertake a dangerous and uncomfortable task as a patriotic duty (because he loved outdoor adventure), yet would often complain petulantly afterwards that his sacrifices were unappreciated.

When he was commissioned a lieutenant colonel, he was sent into the Ohio Valley with militia and British troops to build a fort against the French. His baptism by fire came on July 4, 1754, when the French attacked and compelled them to surrender. They were released upon a pledge to build no more forts on the Ohio for a year.

It was the start of the French and Indian wars. In 1755 George, now a colonel, fought at the side of General Edward Braddock and the British forces in America. Braddock was killed when they were ambushed in the bloody Battle of the Wilderness. Two horses were shot from under George, and four bullets tore through his clothes. Coolly leading a skillful retreat, he saved the army from annihilation. At twenty-three he became Commander of all Virginia troops.

Years of roughing it in the wilderness on an inadequate diet undermined his health. He lost his teeth and required dentures, which were made for him later in Boston by Paul Revere. Once he was so ill that the rumor spread that he had died. Upon writing to a friend, he received a startled reply: "I have heard of letters from the dead, but never had the pleasure of receiving one till yours came to hand the other day."

In January 1759 he remedied both his loneliness and modest circumstances at one stroke by marrying a wealthy widow, the agreeable Martha Dandridge Custis. Now he owned over a hundred slaves, and also hired blacksmiths, carpenters, millers, and weavers. He used them to make Mount Vernon an almost self-sufficient community, because he was too far from towns to supply his needs adequately.

Elected to the House of Burgesses, he became careful that his dress should identify him promptly as a Virginia gentleman, and not as a crude backwoodsman. In one order to London he required "a superfine blue broadcloth coat with silver trimmings . . . a fine scarlet waistcoat, full laced . . . silver lace for a hat . . . and six pairs of the very neatest shoes."

He was wholly shocked when the Townshend Acts were passed, writing Virginia statesman George Mason, "Our lordly masters in Great Britain will be satisfied with nothing less than the deprivation of American freedom." Virginians must, he said, "maintain the liberty which we have derived from our ancestors. . . . No man should scruple or hesitate a moment to use arms in defense of so valuable a blessing."

But only, he added cautiously, as a "last resort."

At first he saw nothing inconsistent in demanding freedom for white colonists while denying it to his slaves. He did not frankly admit, as Patrick Henry did, that he needed slaves to operate his plantations profitably. He saw himself as a humanitarian because he supported more slaves than he needed, refusing to sell any without their permission or turn them out without any means of support.

But a Polish visitor to Mount Vernon noted that the huts of his slaves were "more miserable than the most miserable cottages of our peasants. The husband and wife sleep on a mean pallet, the children on the ground."

George's view of his slaves was altered, however, by his involvement with the radicals. Influenced by their democratic visions, he grew to feel that slavery was wrong, and joined those who demanded abolition of the slave trade.

When the House of Burgesses was shut down in May 1774, George was one of the Virginia radicals who met in the Raleigh Tavern to vow support for New England's resistance to Crown tyranny. "If need be," he promised, "I will raise one thousand men, subsist them at my own expense, and march myself at their head to the relief of Boston."

Elected a delegate to the First Continental Congress, he created a stir by taking his seat in full militia uniform, indicating to other delegates that he was even now ready to take the field if necessary. When conservatives insisted that the Congress instead make fresh appeals to the King, George wrote home impatiently, "Shall we, after this, whine and cry for relief when we have already tried in vain?"

Visiting John Adams and Richard Henry Lee in their lodgings, he appealed to them privately not to press for Independence. Such a course, he warned, would mean "the loss of those valuable rights and privileges . . . without which life, liberty and property are rendered totally insecure."

At the Second Congress in 1775, when the question of choosing a Commander-in-Chief arose, all eyes turned to the huge Virginian in the brilliant uniform of the Virginia militia—a blue and buff coat with rich gold epaulets, elegant sword and black badge on his hat. Of all Americans he had the most celebrated military reputation. Besides, both Adamses were determined to strengthen the ties of the South to New England by putting a Virginian in command of the Continental forces. Trusting George as a patriot, they also counted on his wealth and aristocratic dignity to lend prestige to the Army, and reassure conservative delegates that it would not become a rabble.

But George was not eager for the honor, well aware of what it was likely to cost him. "From the day I enter upon the command of the American armies," he sighed to Patrick Henry, "I date my fall and the ruin of my reputation." He knew that he would be mercilessly criticized on all sides both for what he did with the little given him, and even more for what he would be unable to do.

Troubled and serious, he nevertheless accepted, declaring that he would serve without compensation. "I beg it be remembered by every gentleman in this room," he added gravely, "that I this declare with the utmost sincerity, I do not think myself equal to the Command I am honored with."

Many in the room soon grew convinced he was right.

Reaching Cambridge after the battle of Bunker Hill and the burning of Charlestown, he took command of the colonial forces—fifteen thousand untrained, ruggedly individualistic farmers and town boys, many without weapons, with whom he was expected to drive the British out of Boston.

He deplored their lack of discipline. They resented taking orders that they had no voice in framing, and objected fiercely to punishment for leaving a guard post, drunkenness, discourtesy to officers, or sleeping on duty. Weren't they all volunteers fighting against tyranny? Then why should they submit to being tyrannized by fellow Americans? "They regarded an officer," George complained, "no more than a broomstick."

He spent eight months trying to train his unruly army, most of whom saw no reason not to return home whenever there was a military lull. Like many of the Southern aristocracy, George took a snobbish view toward the "common" New Englanders. When the New England leaders discovered George's prejudice they were outraged.

Their anger chastened George, who became more discreet in what he said and wrote. That became apparent when he received a poem from a young black New England poet, Phyllis Wheatley. The Yankee-scorning slave holder replied respectfully, "If you should ever come to Cambridge . . . I shall be happy to see a person so favored by the Muses, and to whom nature has been so liberal and beneficent."

The irritations between George and the New Englanders were submerged when the British shelled and burned Falmouth in October for "most unpardonable rebellion."

He was faced with a fresh problem in December when most enlistments expired. Walking among his troops, George begged them not to quit and go home because their country needed them desperately. Significantly, he dared not suggest a draft to the Congress. Patriotism to most Americans was a voluntary affair; conscription was a European tyranny.

Many volunteers saw little point in staying in uniform. They were so desperately short of powder and cannonballs that when the British fired theirs, the Yankees had to run after them and stockpile them to use in firing back.

"My situation is inexpressibly distressing," George wrote John Hancock desperately, "to see the winter fast approaching upon a naked army, the time of their service within a few weeks of expiring. . . . The Paymaster has not a single dollar in hand. . . . If the evil is not immediately remedied . . . the Army must absolutely break up."

As often as three times a day he sent express riders to Philadelphia begging for clothing, shoes, medicines and ammunition. Delegates called him a nagging pessimist.

George's plight was no secret to the British. Count Rumford, a British officer, called his army "most wretchedly clothed, and as dirty a set of mortals as ever disgraced the name of a soldier. . . . They have no women in the camp to do washing for the men, and . . . [would rather] let their linen, etc., rot upon their backs than to be at the trouble of cleaning 'em themselves. . . . The soldiers in general are most heartily sick of the service, and . . .

cannot bear to be commanded by others that are their superiors in nothing . . . but a superior commission. . . .

Throughout the winter of 1775–76 George was powerless to act against the British in Boston. In February he complained, "So far from my having my army of twenty thousand well-armed, etc., I have been here with less than one half of it, including sick, furloughed . . . and those neither armed nor clothed, as they should be. . . . I have been obliged to use art to conceal it from my own officers."

Finally, in March, General Henry Knox succeeded in dragging fifty captured cannon over the snowy mountains of New England on oxsleds, a 200-mile journey from Ticonderoga, New York, to Cambridge. Overnight George put them in place on Dorchester Heights overlooking south Boston. In the morning he threatened to batter the English position to bits.

General Howe, who had now succeeded Gage in command, took one horrified look through his spyglass and ordered an evacuation of Boston at once. He threatened to burn Boston as he left if George fired on his troops during the evacuation, so the American guns were kept silent. The British sailed out of the harbor on March 17, taking with them a thousand Tory sympathizers. The following day George entered Boston in triumph amid a day of patriot rejoicing.

Elated by his first victory, George now began to have second thoughts about Independence, especially after reading Thomas Paine's pamphlet, *Common Sense,* which had appeared in January.

He discussed the question thoughtfully with leaders of the Congress during the May conference in Philadelphia to which John Hancock had summoned him. With Howe expected to land momentarily in New York with a powerful new army, he revealed the painful news that even with his army now shrunken to ten thousand men, he had only 6,641 present and fit for duty, the rest sick, on furlough, or absent without leave.

He sped to New York just before Howe landed, but only in time to retreat with his forces before smashing attacks. His army melted away as he fell back into New Jersey, then toward Delaware. Faced with the bleak prospect of annihilation or surrender, George heard that Richard Henry Lee had voiced Virginia's demand for proclaiming Independence.

Independence now? Dear God, if they couldn't defend themselves as British colonists, with some support from sympathetic English cousins, how in the world could they ever hope to do so as an enemy nation of Americans?

NINE

The Secret of
Martha Washington

When Martha Washington reached Philadelphia on her way to join her husband at Cambridge in the winter of 1775–76, Dolly Hancock paid a courtesy call. The two women did not get along too well, perhaps because Dolly, like her husband, resented the failure of the Congress to make John Hancock Commander-in-Chief instead of George Washington.

Dolly confided with poisonous sweetness that she was delighted that Martha would soon be joining George, because it would end the "nasty" gossip in Philadelphia that she had chosen to live apart from him because she was Tory in her sympathies. Martha was too shocked to reply. Dolly then went on blandly to observe that she and Martha had a plight in common—having to share their husbands with the country.

By then the usually gentle Martha found her tongue.

"No, Mrs. Hancock," she replied waspishly, "there is a great difference in our situations. Your husband sits in the Congress. Mine fights in the battlefield."

She loved George dearly and was utterly devoted to him—yet she knew that she did not occupy first place in his heart. As a teenager he had become infatuated with Mrs. Sally Fairfax, the slender, flirtatious wife of a neighbor, and he had never gotten over it.

Less than two months after his marriage to Martha, George wrote Sally, "The world has no business to know the object of my love, declared in this manner to you, when I want to conceal it." Nor did he ever lose his infatuation for her. Close to the end of his life, he told Sally that not even the glories of eight years as President "had been able to eradicate from my mind those happy moments, the happiest in my life, which I have enjoyed in your company."

He had married Martha because he couldn't have Sally, because Martha was a great comfort to him, and because her widow's wealth was essential to his plans to make Mount Vernon a great plantation. She may not have realized how he felt about Sally when he married her, but Martha heard the gossip afterwards. If George's secret from her was Sally Fairfax, Martha's secret from him was that she knew.

A planter's daughter, Martha was born on June 2, 1732, in New Kent County, Virginia. Like many "gentlewomen" of the day, she received little formal schooling, her instruction limited to reading, writing, simple sums, embroidery, dancing, and playing the spinet. Unlike Abby Adams, she never educated herself, struggling all her life, even as First Lady, with letters she wrote. Her spelling was so bad that it often obscured her meaning—"nightground" for nightgown, "lenght" for length, "fashonob" for fashionable.

When she was seventeen she married thirty-seven-year-old Daniel Parke Custis. His father died eight days later, leaving them a small fortune. They had four children, two of whom died. After only eight years of marriage Custis died of a heart attack, and his twenty-five-year-old widow inherited a seventeen thousand-acre estate, a huge mansion, and thirty thousand pounds.

In those days young men often married with a practical eye on their future, so it was inevitable that the hazel-eyed, wealthy young widow would have a wide choice of suitors. But the only one who fascinated Martha was George Washington.

She found her heart deeply stirred by the tall soldier who handled horses so beautifully, and whose commanding presence awed even her spoiled children, Jack and Patsy. Finding a gentle kindness in his searching gray-blue eyes, she suspected that the somewhat formal, remote manner of the frontier hero hid a shyness with women.

George found Martha charming. She was no great beauty; her nose was too long for her small mouth in a round face, although her hazel eyes were warm and captivating. She dressed so plainly as a rule that she was sometimes mistaken for her maid, although Abby Adams shrewdly noted later, "That plainness is the best of every article."

When they first met at a dinner, George was suffering from one of his bouts of illness, and she noticed that he ate little, seeming to be in some pain. She whispered to him that taking some wine with his food might make him feel better. When it did, his gaze lingered on her gratefully.

She sensed that he was lonely and needed looking after. She was lonely too, and needed someone to look after. She also missed having a man to cope with the problems and responsibilities of running her large estate.

As for George, he felt comfortable with Martha. She was a cozy, simple person with common sense and no pretensions of intellect, gracious in manner, frank, a good listener, and given to generous impulses. He knew she would make a good wife. Moreover, his Mount Vernon house was then only eight rooms, set in two thousand largely uncultivated acres. It would take much more money than he had to develop it into a prosperous plantation. Marrying Martha would solve that problem.

He proposed the fourth time he saw her, and she happily accepted. They were married on January 6, 1759. The wedding was an elaborate affair attended by magnificently dressed Virginians in powdered wigs, including Governor Fauquier, and ladies in satin and diamond buckles. Martha wore a yellow brocade dress over a white and silver petticoat, lilac silk slippers embroidered in gold and silver, with high heels because George was so tall. Pearls decorated her powdered hair.

They left for a three-month honeymoon in Martha's Williamsburg home. She rode with three bridesmaids in a coach drawn by six horses, while George escorted it on a splendid horse with grand trappings at the head of a cortege.

Afterwards, Martha and the children moved into Mount Vernon. With her fortune behind him, he began to enlarge and improve the plantation while Martha developed the house into a mansion with charming grounds. She had no trouble keeping her mother-in-law at a distance, since that hawk-eyed, domineering matriarch did not care to live at Mount Vernon, much to the relief of George.

Easygoing and flexible in her habits, Martha had only one rigid routine she insisted upon—a morning hour alone in her bedchamber, which no one, including George and the children, was allowed to disturb. During Martha's hour of privacy George would ride around the farms to supervise plantation work.

They generally had company in the afternoons, with dinners at three. Before receiving his guests, George would get out of riding clothes and into a light suit, applying fresh powder to his wig. The first time that Sally Fairfax and her husband were expected at Mount Vernon, Martha was grateful when she observed that George let no word or glance pass between him and Sally, behaving with his usual grave courtesy and calm.

For this public loyalty to her, Martha gave him her serene understanding and trust. More than that, she made Mount Vernon a pleasant paradise for him, seeing to it that he had every comfort and all the companionship he needed. A popular hostess, she was pleasant, yet unpretentious, with a knack for making their guests feel at home. Unlike Abby, she could not converse with them about politics or books— she almost never read one—but she delighted their palates with marvelous cooking. Her recipes were in great demand by other wives.

George was an equally cordial host—too much of a Virginia gentleman to swear or use tobacco—but he was no Puritan like Sam and John Adams. He gambled mildly and drank socially with his friends. Martha learned that he had a furious temper, but almost always kept it under magnificent control, earning a reputation for unshakable calm and poise.

Her world now centered wholly on him, her two children, and Mount Vernon, which she governed with a ring of keys hanging at her side. It was George, however, who really managed everything. Martha, noted one historian, was "rather inclined to leave the matter under her husband's control."

The children were delighted with their new father. He was fond of them too, and encouraged them to call him Papa. But he felt that Martha spoiled them outrageously. When he sought to discipline them, she would not allow it, once reminding him tartly that they were her children, not his.

A year after their marriage, Martha had caught the measles, which may possibly have affected her ability to have any children with George. In any event, none were born, much to their regret. Martha worried that it might hurt his affection for her, but he never expressed his disappointment.

Martha was grief-stricken in 1773 when seventeen-year-old Patsy died of epilepsy. George was equally saddened by the loss. When Jack turned eighteen and took young Nelly Calvert as his bride, Martha and George urged the newlyweds to live at Mount Vernon. "My dear Nelly," Martha wrote, "God took from me a daughter when June roses were blooming. He has now given me another daughter, about her age when winter winds are blowing, to warm my heart again." Touched, Nelly came to Mount Vernon and was soon deeply attached to her mother-in-law.

In September 1774 Martha was unhappy when George invited Patrick Henry to spend the night. She disliked Henry, considering him an uncouth radical whose backwoodsman talk and swagger, she suspected, was a pose. But the reason for her melancholy was that in the morning George and Henry were riding off together to the First Continental Congress in Philadelphia for no one knew how long.

After they had left, while entertaining Virginia statesman Edward Pendleton and other guests, Martha learned about George's vow at the Williamsburg Convention to raise a thousand men and march them to the relief of Boston if necessary. She felt proud at their praise of him, yet frightened. If George tried to lead untrained civilians against the King's crack regiments, she knew there was a very good chance that she would be forced to wear widow's weeds again.

Yet she hid her fears so well that Pendleton, in a letter describing his visit, wrote, "I was much pleased with Mrs. Washington and her spirit. She seemed ready to make any sacrifice and was very cheerful, though I know she felt anxious. She talked like a Spartan mother to her son going into battle. 'I hope you will stand firm—I know George will,' she said."

Although she sympathized with the American cause, Martha was not too happy about the radical hotheads who wanted to rush to war with England over it. Soon after George returned from Philadelphia he told her about Patrick Henry's "liberty or death" speech at the Richmond Convention. Henry, George sighed ruefully, was obviously spoiling for a fight.

"Yes," Martha said tartly, "because his experience of combat is exactly the same as mine." If it came to a fight, she knew, her husband would be in the front lines while Patrick Henry would be making a fire-eating speech in some hall.

If the trouble with England worsened, she was resigned to the knowledge that George would be chosen to lead any resistance in Virginia. But it came as a distinct shock when she heard the news of George's nomination as Commander-in-Chief.

He knew it would be. He wrote her a painful letter of apology for having accepted the post that would take him so far away from her: "My Dearest. . . . So far from seeking this appointment, I have used every endeavor in my power to avoid it, not only from my unwillingness to part with you and the family, but from a consciousness of its being a trust too great for my capacity. . . . I should enjoy more real happiness in one month with you at home. . . . It was utterly out of my power to refuse. . . . I therefore beg that you will summon your whole fortitude, and pass your time as agreeably as possible . . . as it must add greatly to my uneasy feelings to hear that you are dissatisfied or complaining at what I really could not avoid."

Worried about her, he urged Jack and Nelly, who had left Mount Vernon, to return and keep Martha from missing him too much. "I think it absolutely necessary," George wrote his stepson, "for the peace and satisfaction of your mother."

Now Martha's daily anxiety for George's safety made her eager for every scrap of news about the fortunes of the Americans in arms. If they lost the contest with England, she knew, even if George survived battle he would end up on the gallows as a traitor to the Crown. This harrowing worry haunted her sleepless nights. Yet never once did she write urging that some way be found to end the struggle. If liberty was George's cause, it was her cause too.

When Governor Dunmore burned Norfolk, word spread that Martha was in danger of being seized as a hostage. Virginia radicals urged her to leave the colony at once, but she refused. She agreed with George, who wrote his cousin Lund Washington, "I can hardly think that Lord Dunmore can act so low and unmanly a part as to think of seizing Mrs. Washington by way of revenge on me."

George counted hopefully on returning to her that winter, but by October 1775 he realized that he would have to stay on in the field outside Boston. Missing her deeply, he now urged her to come north to him instead. The message filled Martha with joy. She was enraptured at the thought of being reunited with him soon, even if it meant living within sight and sound of the enemy's guns.

Undaunted by the prospect of venturing far beyond the restricted world of the plantation lady, she ordered her trunks packed for an immediate departure. Jack and Nelly insisted upon accompanying her, asking for a twenty-four-hour delay to prepare. Martha would not hear of it, and they were forced to set out with her almost at once on the difficult 1,100-mile winter journey north to Cambridge.

Both entering and leaving Philadelphia she was escorted by militia with great pomp—"as if I had been a very great some-body," she wrote a friend in amusement.

Reunited happily with George after a seven-month separation, Martha assumed her role as hostess of Craigie House, his yellow brick headquarters. His officers and their wives quickly felt at ease with her. Martha organized a sewing and knitting circle to mend for Army bachelors, and another to roll bandages for the hospital just across the road.

"Some days we have a number of cannon and shells from Boston and Bunkers Hill," she wrote home to a friend, "but it does not seem to surprise anyone but me; I confess I shudder every time I hear the sound of a gun. . . . The preparations are very terrible indeed, but I endeavor to keep my fears to myself as well as I can."

Happy to be with George, she determined never to be separated from him for long again, no matter what length of time the war took or what rigors she had to endure. From then on for eight years she was to follow wherever the fortunes of war took him, to the delight of his men. She always arrived in winter encampments in a coach filled with food so that, as an old journal noted, "Her arrivals at camp were events much anticipated by the soldiers."

In one village where only a crude dwelling was available as shelter for the General and his lady, two village youths were given the task of making it livable. Martha brought them each a glass of wine as they worked, and praised them for "masterly work"— she whose own home was furnished with exquisite, imported furnishings. Then she sat them down at the Washingtons' table and served their meals. "We studied to do everything," said one, "to please so pleasant a lady."

As for the danger, Martha preferred to share it with George than fret about it at home. Unspoiled by the riches she had grown accustomed to, she even found herself enjoying the Spartan life of a soldier's wife. She told her husband that she "preferred the sound of fifes and drums . . . to any music that was ever heard."

Having her near him was a tremendous comfort to George. It did not matter to him now that she was only a small, plump, simply-dressed middle-aged woman. She looked after him with motherly care, and he found her company vastly calming and reassuring. In the midst of the hurly-burly and uncertainties of the struggle, Martha Washington was the rock of stability her husband needed in his darkest moments of despair.

She often helped him by making copies of his General Orders for his various generals, happy to ease some of the burden of crushing responsibility her husband carried.

Early in 1776 Martha had her portrait painted in a miniature on ivory, and presented it to George as a keepsake. It showed her with a quiet smile, her hazel eyes warm and candid, as though expressing pride and confidence in her husband. If George still carried Sally Fairfax's image in his heart romantically, he wore Martha's portrait in a gold locket around his neck throughout the war. The deep affection he bore her grew stronger through the years.

When George had to leave for New York, Martha insisted on joining him there despite the grave danger of imminent invasion by Howe's forces. After John Hancock called George to Philadelphia for an urgent conference, Martha made the journey with him, although smallpox inoculations had left her so feverish that she was forced to bed when they arrived.

She was still ailing when George had to rush back to New York. So on June 7, when Richard Henry Lee stood up in his light summer suit to read the Resolution for Independence, Martha wrote her husband from her sickbed all that she heard about the raging debate that followed.

If there was the smallest thing she could do for the husband on whose shoulders rested the fate of the thirteen colonies, Martha Washington never left it undone.

TEN

The Silver-Tongued Bumpkin:

Patrick Henry

Even after he had become a prominent lawyer and legislator, Patrick Henry continued to dress like a backwoods rustic, more concerned with improving his mind than his appearance. A friend warned that he was distracting people from what he had to say by the shabby way he looked. Turning to a mirror, he studied his rumpled gray clothes and scowled.

"Here is a coat good enough for me," he muttered, "yet I must get a new one to please the eyes of other people!"

His uncouth appearance so shocked John Randolph, when Patrick first came before the King's attorney general for Virginia to be examined for the bar, that Randolph at first refused to consider him. Finally persuaded to do so, the aristocrat sought to get rid of Patrick swiftly by posing complicated legal problems and misleading him about the answers. Patrick didn't know the actual law involved, but shrewdly disputed him with arguments based on common sense. Astonished, Randolph took down law books and showed him the official verdicts.

"You have never seen these books . . . yet you are right!" he marveled. Apologizing for having judged a man by appearances, Randolph said warmly, "Mr. Henry, if your industry be only half equal to your genius . . . you will do well, and become an ornament and an honor to your profession."

An outlandish accent led Patrick to pronounce China "Cheena," earth "yearth," natural "naiteral" and learning "larnin'," yet such was the magic of his tongue that when he used it in oratory the effects were miraculous. Virginia statesman George Mason said admiringly that, had Patrick lived in ancient Rome, the people would have made him First Consul of the Republic.

A superb actor, he rooted people to their seats in fascination as his words fell into an utterly hushed room, now rolling like thunder, now whispered softly. Sometimes tears of ecstasy streamed down his cheeks as his voice rang out in defense of the people's rights. Reporting his effect upon all in a courtroom, one spellbound observer noted, "He made their blood run cold, and their hair to rise on end."

Despite his brilliance, many considered Patrick Henry a lazy, crude loafer and ne'er-do-well. Even when the courts were in session, he would often head off into the woods for weeks of deerhunting with cronies, never taking the clothes off his back as he camped in the forests.

Henry was born in Hanover County, Virginia, on May 29, 1736, son of a frontier farmer, Scotsman John Henry. As a schoolboy he was a day-dreamer who often deserted his books for fishing rod and shotgun. He loved to roam the woods and riverbanks in sloppy clothes—"to learn the language of the birds," he once said seriously. His favorite companions were trappers and frontiersmen.

Annoyed by his son's truancy, John Henry took over Patrick's education when he was eleven, aided by the boy's clergyman uncle. Between them they managed to cram some degree of reading, writing, mathematics, Latin, and Greek into the reluctant Patrick's head during the next four years.

At fifteen he was apprenticed to a country merchant for a year, then put to work in a store run by his elder brother William. One day a customer entered to find Patrick stretched out full length bantering with cronies. Asked for salt Patrick drawled, "Just sold the last peck," and continued his small talk—while lying on a sack of salt.

He was equally indifferent to collecting bills owed the store, preferring to slip away to the woods and play the flute. Since his brother was just as disinterested in hard work as Patrick, the store went bankrupt in a year.

When he was eighteen, the improvident Patrick exasperated his father further by taking a wife—Sarah Shelton, daughter of a small farmer who afterwards opened a tavern. The newlyweds persuaded both fathers to help them, and were staked to a small farm with half a dozen slaves to work it. Within two years Patrick proved as hopeless a farmer as he had been a merchant and was forced to sell out. With the money he opened his own country store, spending most of his time in idle conversation with cronies. Three years later, at twenty-three, Patrick was once more broke and out of business, with a growing family to support.

Thomas Jefferson met him at a dance at the home of a Virginia colonel three years later. "Mr. Henry had, a little before, broken up his store," Jefferson recalled, "or rather it had broken him up; but his misfortunes were not to be traced either in his countenance or conduct. . . . His manners had something of coarseness in them. His passion was music, dancing and pleasantry. He excelled in the last, and it attached everyone to him." Dismal failure he might be, but he was such a carefree companion of contagious good cheer that Patrick made friends wherever he went.

His ability to speak brilliantly amazed many, including Jefferson, who told Daniel Webster, "He was a man of very little knowledge of any sort . . . and had no books. . . . I have been often astonished at his command of proper language; how he obtained the knowledge of it I never could find out, as he read little, and conversed little with educated men."

Puzzling over how to make a living, Patrick hit on the idea of becoming a lawyer. Because of his allergy to books, his ambition at first seemed absurd to his father. But Patrick felt that years of idle chatter with country store and tavern loafers had made him a skillful debater. He had learned how to excite men, how to make them laugh or sigh, how to change their views. Moreover, his own hard luck had made him compassionate toward people in trouble, especially underdogs with little chance in legal struggles against the powerful rich.

Even after he had won admission to the bar, however, it was not easy for an unknown young lawyer to attract clients. Patrick was compelled to operate his practice out of the tavern his father-in-law opened in Hanover, where he helped out as bartender and desk clerk. For three or four years Patrick despaired of practicing much at any bar except the one in his father-in-law's tavern.

His first real opportunity came in what became known as "the Parsons' Cause," a lawsuit brought by the ministers of Virginia, who complained that they were not being paid enough out of public taxes. The people engaged Patrick to oppose the Crown-supported clergy. When his clergyman uncle sought to attend court to hear him, Patrick begged him not to.

"Your appearance there might strike me with such awe," he said, "as to prevent me from doing justice to my clients."

At the trial he made a fierce attack on the clergy for neglecting their duties. "Do they feed the hungry and clothe the naked?" he demanded. "Oh, no, gentlemen! . . . These rapacious harpies . . . would snatch from the hearth of their honest parishioner his last hoe-cake, from the widow and her orphaned children her last milch-cow!"

His castigation grew so scathing that the clergymen present could bear no more and fled the courtroom in embarrassment. Patrick thundered that the King had forfeited the right to obedience from Virginians by supporting the clergy's claims against the people, in opposition to their representatives, and so had become a tyrant.

There were indignant cries of "Treason! Treason!" But the courtroom shook with applause. The jury awarded the clergy the sum of one penny, and the jubilant people carried Patrick Henry from the courtroom on their shoulders.

When his uncle reproached him for having opposed the clergy, he shrugged that since the clergy had not seen fit to hire him, he saw no reason why their opponents shouldn't. Besides, he added practically, he needed important cases like this one to make his reputation. And that is precisely what the Parsons' Cause did. His eloquence on behalf of popular government against Crown rule won him wide attention.

When the Stamp Act agitated Virginians, a member of the House of Burgesses resigned his seat in favor of Patrick so that the silver-tongued orator could lead an attack on the tax. As he rose to speak, rich landowners who supported the Crown made mocking comments about his uncouth appearance and manner. Their smiles quickly turned to alarmed scowls.

On fire with emotion, he denounced the right of Parliament to levy taxes on Virginians without their consent and proposed that they defy any such law, branding any Virginian who obeyed it an enemy of the colony. He boldly warned the King, "Caesar had his Brutus—Charles the First, his Cromwell—and George the Third . . ."

The House fell into uproar. "Treason! Treason!"

". . . may profit by their example," finished Patrick defiantly. "If *this* be treason, make the most of it!"

The outraged Speaker of the House wrathfully reproached its members for not having stopped Henry from making so disloyal a speech. Patrick rose again to apologize for giving offense, discreetly vowing his loyalty to King George to the last drop of his blood. Having his country's dying liberties at heart, he said, he had simply been carried away in the heat of passion. When other members rose to defend him, the disgruntled Speaker decided to accept Patrick's apology.

His proposals—the Virginia Resolves—carried by the narrow margin of one vote. Shocked, Peyton Randolph rushed out of the hall crying in frustration, "By God, I would give five hundred guineas for a single vote!"

For some Americans, Patrick's defiance of England marked the real beginning of the American Revolution. The Governor of Massachusetts called the Virginia Resolves an "alarm bell" ringing out to summon Americans to defend their liberties. New York found the Resolves so treasonable that they refused to print them.

The Virginia Resolves propelled Patrick to leadership of the radical party in Virginia, and also brought him more law clients than he could handle. Now triumphant over the aristocrats who had mocked his rusticity, he did not hesitate to pay them back. One day, entering a store in Williamsburg, he observed a conservative rival deeply absorbed in a book of ancient history. "What, Mr. Wormley, still studying books?" he chuckled insolently. "Study men, Mr. Wormley, study men!"

He was now financially able to move his family out of his father-in-law's tavern and into an estate of his own with slaves.

"Would anyone believe I am the master of slaves of my own purchase!" he wrote a friend wryly. "I am drawn along by the general inconvenience of living here without them. I will not, I cannot justify it. . . . I believe a time will come when an opportunity will be offered to abolish this lamentable evil. . . . Let us transmit to our descendants, together with our slaves, a pity for their unhappy lot and an abhorrence of slavery." Yet, significantly, he preferred the comforts provided by slave labor to living by his principles.

More and more he became the artful actor, developing his dramatic ability. He used captivating gestures, let smiles play about his mouth, flashed his deep-set, sky-blue eyes with such brilliance that people talked of "the Patrick flash." He was now a hollow-cheeked, lantern-jawed, slightly stooped six-footer with a straight Roman nose that jutted out from a high forehead like the prow of a narrow ship plying through heavy seas.

Elected a delegate to the First Continental Congress, to which he rode with George Washington, he found that great things were expected of him. One delegate had said, "Patrick Henry is a moderate and mild man, but the very devil in politics—a son of thunder. He will shake the Congress!"

A debate erupted over whether radical delegates who disagreed with the conservative majority of a delegation should be free to vote with the radicals of other colonies, or whether only the majority vote should count. Patrick argued that voting should represent the people at large, and should not lock delegates into colonial compartments.

He cried, "The distinctions between Virginians, Pennsylvanians, New Yorkers and New Englanders are no more. I am not a Virginian, but an American." And he concluded, "All distinctions are thrown down. All America is one mass!"

It was a strong breath of democracy, the first keynote struck that visualized a free American nation. Such swift strides were much too fast for most delegates, however, who decreed that the Congress should vote by colonies, not delegates.

But after Patrick's speech, Maryland's Samuel Chase was so awed that he told one colleague, "We might as well go home. We aren't able to hold a candle to these Virginians!"

When the First Congress adjourned, Henry returned to Virginia to attend the illegal session of the House of Burgesses that met in March 1775. After listening to Virginia conservatives urge loyalty to the Crown, he rose and began speaking with controlled calm.

"Shall we try argument?" he asked. "Sir, we have been trying that for the last ten years. . . . We have petitioned, we have remonstrated, we have supplicated, we have prostrated ourselves before the throne." His voice began to shake with emotion. "There is no longer any room for hope. . . . We must fight! . . . They tell us, sir, that we are weak—unable to cope with so formidable an adversary. But when shall we be stronger? . . . Three millions of people, armed in the holy cause of liberty . . . are invincible!"

Now his vibrating oratory seemed to rock the hall as his face grew pale, his neck tendons stood out like whipcords, and his eyes glared terribly. "There is no retreat but in submission and slavery! Our chains are forged! Their clanking may be heard on the plains of Boston! The war is inevitable—and let it come! I repeat, sir, *let it come!*"

As excitement swept his audience, he leveled an accusing finger. "Gentlemen may cry peace, peace—but there *is* no peace! The war is actually begun! The next gale that sweeps from the north will bring to our ears the clash of resounding arms! Our brethren are already in the field! Why stand we idle here?" Crossing his wrists as though manacled, he pantomimed a forlorn prisoner in a dungeon.

"Is life so dear, or peace so sweet, as to be purchased at the price of chains and slavery?" He lifted his "chained" hands toward heaven. "Forbid it, Almighty God!" Straightening, erect and defiant, he "broke" his chains by hurling his arms apart. "I know not what course others may take; but as for me, give me *liberty* . . . or give me *death!*"

His fist at his left breast as though clutching a dagger in his heart, he stood there rigidly, white-faced, trembling with emotion. There was no applause, no cries of treason—only a profound, shocked silence.

Then, suddenly, the assembly burst into a deafening uproar. Enthusiastic legislators voted swift approval of Patrick's resolution to organize and train a Virginia militia. He was named to head the organizing committee, which included Washington, Jefferson, and Richard Henry Lee. Soon hunting shirts inscribed "Liberty or Death" were seen all over Virginia.

Governor Dunmore landed a squad of marines from a British warship under cover of darkness, marched them into Williamsburg, and carried off all the powder in the city magazine. Now let Patrick Henry's rebels try to start trouble!

The alarm spread, and with it public indignation. Gathering the citizens of Hanover, Patrick led them toward the capital for a showdown with the Governor. Five thousand more Virginians sprang to arms. Alarmed, Dunmore intercepted them with an emissary who offered them more money than the powder had been worth. Patrick accepted for the citizens, and the money was used to order more powder from other colonies. But some radicals criticized Patrick for accepting the settlement, instead of marching on to Williamsburg and sweeping the Crown government out of Virginia.

By now, however, Patrick knew his Virginians too well to risk moving too fast. They would support his oratory, but only a handful were yet ready for open revolution. The chief value of the incident was that it had served to infuriate and unite Virginians against Crown attempts to intimidate them.

"You may in vain mention to them the duties on tea . . ." he said "But tell them of the robbery of the magazine, and that the next step will be to disarm them, and they will be then ready to fly to arms to defend themselves."

When things calmed down momentarily, Dunmore issued an angry proclamation against "a certain Patrick Henry . . . and a number of deluded followers" who had "put themselves in a posture of war . . . exciting the people to join in these outrageous practises." He called on all loyal Virginians to oppose Patrick "by every means" before an indignant King George punished them as the rebellious Bostonians had been punished.

Three days later Patrick prudently left Virginia for the Second Continental Congress, escorted by armed guards ready to fight off the Governor's men if any attempt were made to seize him as a traitor.

He was more chary now of making flamboyant speeches to the new Congress. Jefferson explained why: "He had the good sense to perceive that his declamation, however excellent in its proper place, had no weight at all in such an assembly as that of cool-headed, reflecting, judicious men. . . . He seemed, indeed, very tired of the place, and wonderfully relieved when, by appointment of the Virginia Convention to be Colonel of their first regiment, he was permitted to leave Congress about the last of July."

Back in Virginia, he proved enormously popular with his men because of his democratic ideas of command. He saw no reason why volunteers should have to obey or salute officers. Why should men banded together to fight for freedom be divided into superiors and inferiors?

The military men of Virginia were horrified. Even Patrick's friend Washington wrote ruefully from Cambridge, "I think my countrymen made a capital mistake when they took Henry out of the senate to place him in the field."

Virginia's Committee of Safety did not deny Patrick's courage or eagerness to fight, but warned that if his undisciplined regiment had to fight the British, it would be slaughtered. He refused to listen. He would show King George how brave, dedicated men fought when united as free equals, instead of manipulated as tin soldiers!

But the Committee of Safety appointed a general over his head. Outraged, Patrick promptly resigned and returned home, to discover that his wife Sarah had just died. Deeply depressed, he stayed home for some months to care for his six children.

Now, at forty, Patrick was out of the Army, out of Congress, out of public life, watching helplessly from the sidelines as Howe's military successes imperiled the American cause. He became convinced that the Congress must be made to issue a Declaration of Independence at once, form a confederation, and as a new nation win aid from France. "Delay may bring on us total ruin," he wrote anxiously to Richard Henry Lee.

Winning election as a delegate to the Virginia Convention that met on May 6, 1775, in Williamsburg, Patrick attended wearing buckskin clothes, yarn stockings, and an unpowdered wig. He quickly overwhelmed the delegates by the power of his oratory, and on May 15 the Convention voted to instruct its delegates in Philadelphia to propose an immediate Declaration of Independence, followed promptly by organization of a national union with local self-government for each state.

So it was Patrick Henry's eloquent voice that finally began turning the wheels of liberty by causing Richard Henry Lee to rise in the Congress to propose freedom.

John Adams noted enthusiastically that Patrick, as the author of the Virginia Resolves, and now of the proposal for Independence, deserved to "have the glory with posterity of beginning and conducting this great revolution."

That wasn't bad for a backwoods bumpkin.

ELEVEN

The Man of Common Sense:
Thomas Paine

He had no lack of enemies. After the Revolution when he visited England, mobs burned his books, hung him in effigy, painted his name on their shoe soles so they could step on him, set fire to the homes of any seen associating with him, and forced him to fly to France. There he was flung into jail, and the President he had fought under in the Revolution refused to get him out because he had attacked organized religion, whereupon he bitterly attacked George Washington as "a hypocrite in public life."

Freed from his French dungeon through the efforts of James Monroe, he returned home to be cursed openly in the streets. Mobs gathered to jeer at him. Stagecoach owners refused to transport him. Election supervisors challenged his right to vote. Federalist editors demanded that the "loathe-some reptile" and "lying, drunken, brutal infidel" be hanged.

As he lay dying in poverty, angry crowds gathered outside shouting demands that he repent his blasphemies. After his death the usually-tolerant Quakers refused to bury him in a Quaker cemetery. Historians then sought to keep his name as much as possible out of histories of the Revolution.

He was born in England at Thetford, Norfolk, son of a Quaker corsetmaker, on January 29, 1737. Like Patrick Henry and Sam Adams, he seemed born to failure. After a grammar school education and two years at sea on the crew of a privateer, he became a tax collector but was fired for being too softhearted. When he opened a tobacconist's shop, it did poorly because he was far more preoccupied with studying great writers.

He also attended science lectures, and began corresponding with the London agent for the colony of Pennsylvania, Benjamin Franklin, about the latter's electricity experiments.

The shop failed and Thomas fled into hiding to escape debtors' prison. Given a second chance as a tax collector, he was fired again, this time for writing the grievances of his fellow collectors in an eloquent petition to Parliament.

To add to his troubles, a first wife died in childbirth and a second wife left him. Despairing of ever rising out of his wretched life as long as he remained in England, Thomas determined to seek a fresh start in the colonies. He called upon Franklin to ask for help.

Franklin saw a hungry-looking man with a long, thin nose, high forehead, sensitive mouth, and large eyes like fiery coals. Impressed with Thomas's intellect, Franklin generously helped pay his passage to Philadelphia and gave him a letter of recommendation to his son-in-law.

Thomas was thirty-seven when he arrived in America in November 1774. Franklin's letter won him a job as editor of the monthly *Pennsylvania Magazine*—the first success of his life. In less than two years his views were the talk of the colonies. Many were scandalized, many delighted, by his demands for better treatment of wives, rights for labor, political and economic freedom, and limitation of royal power.

Thomas Paine loved the New World as much as he hated the old. He had little reason to feel patriotic toward England or King George III.

He smoldered with rage over Britain's attempts to tax the colonies, and was even more infuriated by the use of military might to enforce the taxes. Although he was only a new American, he felt more deeply about these outrages than most native patriots themselves.

As he explained it, "When the country into which I had just set my foot was set on fire about my ears, it was time to stir. . . . In a country wherein all men were once adventurers, the difference of a few years in their arrival could make none in their rights."

Acting as a gadfly to American discontent with King George III, Thomas was supremely indifferent to his tiny salary and one cramped room. He worked persistently toward a goal that fired him with zeal—Independence. There is some evidence to suggest that he was encouraged in this respect by token sums secretly paid him by an agent of King Louis XVI of France, who was not at all loath to see his enemy England harassed by an American revolution.

The conservative publisher of the *Pennsylvania Magazine* put up with the firebrand editor because Thomas's ability to provoke controversy had won many new readers. But when he used its columns to suggest that revolution might be the answer to problems with the English, the publisher fired him.

Undaunted, Thomas decided to make a bold, outright appeal for revolution, and not just to Pennsylvanians but to all Americans. He spent most of the autumn of 1775 writing a passionate yet reasoned appeal for Independence, which he at first called *Plain Truth.*

How could Americans pretend to be loyal to the King while fighting his troops on American soil? He urged fellow colonies to rethink their habit of bowing to the Crown. If they broke with England now, France would give them the foreign aid they needed to win their freedom. And he wound up his powerful appeal by calling boldly for "THE FREE AND INDEPENDENT STATES OF AMERICA."

He showed it to a leading radical, Dr. Benjamin Rush, a subsequent signer of the Declaration. Rush was enthusiastic. Suggesting that the title be changed to *Common Sense,* he told Thomas he believed it would win over America's hesitating moderates who wanted a compromise with the Crown.

Thomas trudged around Philadelphia until he found a printer who dared print *Common Sense*—for half the profits. The threadbare writer not only agreed, but turned his half over to the cause of revolution. Published on January 10, 1776, at two shillings a copy, it caused an immediate sensation.

Within three months 120,000 copies were sold. It was read and eagerly discussed by cobblers in their shops, bakers at their ovens, teachers in their schools, farmers in their fields, soldiers in their camps, delegates at the Congress. Illiterates gathered in groups to hear it read aloud.

"It burst from the press," Rush noted in delight, "with an effect which has rarely been produced by types and paper in any age or country." Radicals laughingly asked any Tory who looked glum if he had "a Paine in his head."

Washington read the pamphlet and a week later wrote to his aide-de-camp Joseph Reed that he was greatly impressed by Thomas Paine's "sound doctrine and unanswerable reasoning." Indicating that it had changed his opinion about Independence, he declared, "If nothing else could satisfy a tyrant and his diabolical ministry, we are determined to shake off all connections with a state so unjust."

Outraged American Loyalists sought to dampen the fiery impact of *Common Sense* by maligning its author. Aristocrats like New York's Governor Morris called Thomas a drunkard, an unscrupulous adventurer from England, a low fellow who dressed filthily and mingled with the lowest trash of the taverns.

But nothing could stop the fuse lit by Thomas from burning ever closer to the explosion point. By turning the idea of Independence from a minority cause of the radicals into a popular idea whose time had come, Thomas Paine paved the way for Richard Henry Lee to toss the bombshell onto the floor of Congress for a decisive vote.

TWELVE

Other Women of '76

Much has been heard of the heroism of the Founding Fathers—but very little about the Founding Mothers.

"The heroism of the females of the Revolution," complained Charles Francis Adams, grandson of John and Abigail, "has gone from memory with the generation that witnessed it, and nothing, absolutely nothing, remains upon the ear of the young of the present day but the faint echo of an expiring general tradition."

In addition to Abby Adams and Martha Washington, there were many lesser-known American women who contributed to making the dream of Independence come true.

Mary Ludwig Hays was a Pennsylvania Dutch girl who accompanied her artilleryman husband John to battle. When he was wounded, she took up his rammer staff, swabbed and loaded his cannon, and helped keep it firing. Coolly, Mary continued fighting on in her husband's place.

Later, when she brought pitcher after pitcher of water to parched troops on a field of battle, she was given the affectionate nickname of "Mollie Pitcher."

Deborah Samson of Plymouth made herself a suit of men's clothing and enlisted in the militia as "Robert Shirtlifee." For three years she served as a common soldier, and was twice wounded. The doctor treating her second wound realized that she was a woman, and sent her to headquarters. Washington himself handed Deborah an honorable discharge, with profound thanks for her unique service to her country.

Teenager Emily Geiger volunteered to carry an urgent written message to a Committee of Safety through an area tightly patrolled by Tories. After riding for two days she was intercepted and detained on suspicion while a matron was sent for to search her. She managed to open and read the message, then shred, chew, and swallow it. When the matron's search revealed nothing, she was freed and rode on to deliver the message verbally.

Many women patriots made brave sacrifices. One British officer sought to intimidate a Mrs. Borden, whose husband and son were with the Continental Army, into cooperating with the Redcoats on pain of having her home burned if she refused.

She handed him a box of matches. "The sight of my house in flames would be a treat for me," she replied, "for I have seen enough to know that you never injure what you have power to keep and enjoy. The application of a torch to my dwelling I should regard as a signal for your depature."

The angry Briton burned her home, then left.

The spirit of such women patriots was expressed by a Philadelphia housewife who wrote in 1776, "Tea I have not drunk since last Christmas, nor bought a new cap or gown. . . . As free I can die but once; but as a slave I shall not be worthy of life. . . . These are the sentiments of all my sister Americans. They have sacrificed assemblies, parties of pleasure, tea drinking and finery, to that great spirit of patriotism. . . . We are making powder fast, and do not want for ammunition."

Many American women did not hesitate to defy British officers to their faces, like Mrs. Daniel Hall. On a visit to her mother in another city, she was stopped by a British officer who demanded the key to her trunk.

"What are you looking for?" she asked.

"For treason, madam," he replied.

"Then you may be saved the trouble of the search, for you may find all you want of it at the end of my tongue!"

After the Minutemen of one Massachusetts community marched off against the British, an alarm spread that Redcoats were approaching from the other side of the Nashua River to take the town. A group of farmers' wives quickly assembled in their husbands' clothes, armed with muskets and pitchforks. Electing Mrs. David Wright of Pepperell their commander, they manned Jewett's Bridge, determined to fight to the death to prevent the British from crossing.

Soon a noted Tory, Captain Leonard Whiting, galloped up on horseback to scout for the British. Mrs. Wright's lady commandoes seized his horse, pulled him out of the saddle, searched him and found incriminating papers. Holding him prisoner, they sent his dispatches by a woman rider to the Committee of Safety.

When the blockade of Boston Harbor caused food shortages in Massachusetts, women patriots took matters into their own hands as greedy Tory merchants sought to hoard food and sell it at exorbitant prices. One day several hundred women descended on a shopkeeper, seizing him and tossing him bodily into a cart. Taking his keys, they "liberated" the scarce commodities in his warehouse. Then they tipped him out of the cart to make room for the groceries, and trundled it off.

It was as much the defiant spirit of American women, as of their husbands, that made possible the momentous day of June 7, 1776, when Richard Henry Lee dared propose Independence to the Second Continental Congress.

THIRTEEN

Grand Climax:

Independence!

England-educated Richard Henry Lee, forty-four, a tall, slim, distinguished figure with copper hair that seemed redder by contrast with his elegant light silk suit, began reading Virginia's proposal in a soft, cultured voice. The left hand with which he gestured was swathed in a black handkerchief to conceal the loss of fingers in an early accident.

An aristocrat who enjoyed fox hunts, he was little interested in the distinguished Lee family's huge tobacco plantations or in his career as a lawyer. What appealed to him most was politics—the opportunity to sway others by his eloquence. He was intensely anti-British because his pride had been wounded by British arrogance toward colonials, especially after having been snubbed in public by General Braddock.

He had made staunch friends and bitter enemies in Virginia. His friends were the radicals like Jefferson and Henry. His enemies were the Tidewater plantation aristocrats among whom he was born and raised, and who considered him a traitor to his class. They had been outraged a dozen years earlier when he had dared challenge and expose the Speaker and treasurer of the House of Burgesses, John Robinson, for secretly lending public funds to his aristocratic cronies.

A stubborn Son of Liberty, he had agreed with Sam Adams about the Stamp Act in 1765; that Americans had to defy it or expect to be saddled with other, worse taxes. "They may take from me one shilling in the pound," he had cried in the Virginia House of Burgesses, "but what security have I for the other nineteen?" He was gleeful whenever Sam or John Adams struck a blow for liberty. "For my part," he wrote, "I must cease to live before I cease to love these proud Patriots."

It was Lee who had suggested to Sam Adams both the Committees of Correspondence in 1772, and the idea of an American union of colonies. He worked with the New Englanders so closely that some resentful Virginians had accused him of representing Massachusetts more than his own colony.

That was why it was he, and not Sam or John Adams, who now stood up to make the proposal that would change the course of American history. The New Englanders trusted Lee, and knew that the explosive resolution would have the best chance of acceptance by all the colonies if it did not come from the hotheaded Yankees but the respectable "gentlemen from Virginia." The aristocratic first colony, and especially the aristocratic Richard Henry Lee, possessed just such respectability.

So now he proposed to a tense Congress "that these United Colonies are, and of right ought to be, free and independent states; that they are absolved from all allegiance to the British Crown; and that all political connection between them and the state of Great Britain is, and ought to be, totally dissolved."

John Adams enthusiastically seconded the motion.

The Congress burst into an uproarious debate that raged on for three days. There was bitter opposition from Maryland, whose legislature had voted unanimously against Independence on the same day Virginia's had voted for it.

Moderate and conservative delegates joined forces to compel a postponement of the motion. Many warned that if the radicals persisted in forcing the issue and won, they would have no alternative but to walk out and go home. This threat to the unity of the colonies forced the radicals to agree to a three-week delay on the vote, to give all sides time to get new instructions from their assemblies at home.

In England, Parliament was ready to concede to the Americans everything they wanted in the way of self-government, except for the making of foreign policy. But because of the great time lag in communications between London and Philadelphia, that news did not reach the colonies in time.

John Adams had a price for the radicals' agreement to a delay on the vote for Independence. If it passed, he pointed out, there would have to be "some sort of a Declaration" to explain it to Americans and the world, and such an important document would take a great while to prepare to the satisfaction of all. So meanwhile why not prepare one "just in case"?

The Congress agreed to appoint a committee for this purpose headed by Thomas Jefferson, and including John Adams, Benjamin Franklin, Connecticut's Roger Sherman, and New York's Robert Livingston. John Adams explained why so young a man as Jefferson had been honored by being named chairman:

"Mr. Jefferson . . . brought with him a reputation for literature, science, and a happy talent of composition. Writings of his were handed about, remarkable for their peculiar felicity of expression."

Meeting with the committee, Thomas suggested that Benjamin Franklin draft the Declaration. Livingston growled that Benjamin couldn't be trusted to resist putting jokes in it. Chuckling, the old sage declined the honor. He had little relish for having his clever phrases skewed and quartered by a Congress full of the nation's sharpest lawyers. Besides, how could anyone write a defense of revolution and Independence that would satisfy both hot radicals and cold conservatives?

Thomas then asked John Adams to do the draft.

John refused, insisting that Thomas write it himself. All on the committee agreed that he was the logical choice. "You are a Virginian," John Adams explained, "and a Virginian ought to appear at the head of this business. Reason second, I am obnoxious, suspected and unpopular. You are very much otherwise. Reason third, you can write ten times better than I can."

"Well," sighed Thomas, "if you are all decided, I will do as well as I can." He saw his task, as he explained later, "to place before mankind the common sense of the subject in terms so plain and firm as to command their assent."

Between June 11 and 28, struggling to keep his thoughts from the ailing wife he loved and worried over, he scribbled away at his portable writing desk in an upstairs room of the bricklayer's house. He tore up page after page as he sought to find the exact words to justify why Americans might vote to tear themselves free from England as a new nation.

While he was writing it, John Adams bustled around to taverns and delegates' lodgings to win votes for Independence with persistent arguments. "I was shunned like a man infected with the leprosy," he recalled later. "I walked the streets of Philadelphia in solitude, borne by the weight of care and unpopularity," But he was determined that somehow, some way, the thirteen colonies must unite on the vote for freedom.

Lobbying just as hard against it was Pennsylvania's John Dickinson, whom John Adams described as "a shadow; tall but slender as a reed; one would think at first sight that he could not live a month."

On June 15 John Adams was overjoyed when the colony of New Jersey went over to the radical position by arresting and ousting the royal Governor, Franklin's natural son William. Benjamin had urged William to resign but his son, a confirmed Tory, had refused. Now they were political enemies.

Thomas Jefferson finished the Declaration in two weeks and showed it first to John Adams, who praised its denunciation of slavery but thought calling the King a tyrant was "too personal." Then Thomas showed it to Franklin, who was confined to his room with gout. Benjamin suggested five changes of phrasing. The full committee then approved the revised document, which was delivered to the Congress on June 28.

It was held aside pending the vote on Independence. If Lee's motion failed, it would simply be tossed into the wastebasket as an exercise in futility. A day later the conservatives had fresh reason to hope that it would be, when the expected British expeditionary armada of fifty-two warships, twenty-seven armed sloops and cutters, and nearly four hundred troop transports arrived in America. In two days the Congress would have to decide whether to defy this mighty army and navy with Washington's pitiful little ragtag army and a few brigs.

As the delegates gathered tensely in the State House on July 1, many were plainly nervous and all were in a state of high suspense. Maryland's fat Samuel Chase, who was mocked behind his back by fellow lawyers as "Bacon-Face," sarcastically accused the radicals of imagining that by uttering the magic word Independence, they could scatter the British fleet.

"If you imagine that I expect the Declaration will ward off calamities from this country," John Adams replied, "you are much mistaken. A bloody conflict we are destined to endure. This has been my opinion from the beginning."

The chief opposition came from Pennsylvania. Of its seven delegates, only Benjamin Franklin and John Morton were liberty men. Most Pennsylvanians felt no immediate threat to themselves, and its leading citizens feared to lose their lands, money, and public office if they defied the Crown. John Dickinson, who led the opposition, argued for delay on grounds that voting for Independence before they even had a government of their own was putting the cart before the horse.

New York's delegates wanted delay too, because their legislature had still sent no instructions. The New Yorkers realized that a vote for Independence meant they would have to bear the brunt of battle with Howe's huge forces. They still hoped for the arrival of a royal peace commission.

The radicals were aware of the grave dangers of a vote for Independence that was not unanimous. Would the colonies that refused to go along switch to England's side and become enemies? John Adams made a long, passionate speech to stir doubtful delegates over to the radical side.

In the midst of it the newly appointed New Jersey delegation arrived, entering the State House drenched from a rainstorm. John broke off his speech and sat down, but New Jersey Judge Richard Stockton asked to hear the arguments for and against Independence before his delegation had to vote.

No one spoke but all eyes turned toward John. Edward Rutledge said to him, "Nobody will speak but you upon this subject. You have all the topics so ready that you must satisfy the gentlemen from New Jersey." So John rose again and summarized the radical position. Then New York's Joseph Alsop rose to denounce Independence in abusive language.

The opinion of the New Jersey delegates was voiced by Princeton President John Witherspoon. "The distinguished gentleman from Massachusetts," he said, "remarked as we came in that the colonies were ripe for Independence." Then he glowered at Joseph Alsop. "I would like to add that some colonies are rotten for the want of it!"

The vote was called with the Congress acting as a "Committee of the Whole"—in effect, a preliminary test vote as preparation for an official, binding vote.

Independence won by a vote of nine colonies to two. Only Pennsylvania and South Carolina voted against. New York had abstained, lacking instructions. Only two of Delaware's three delegates were present, and they were split.

John Hancock adjourned the meeting until the following morning, when the final vote would be taken. The delay was important because it would allow the four delegates that had not voted for Independence to decide whether to cast their lot with the majority, or be left out of the new American Union.

The Delaware delegate who favored Independence, Thomas McKean, vowed to get Ceasar Rodney back to Congress to vote Delaware for Independence "if I have to travel to Dover myself after supper and bring him back, riding pillion [two on a horse] by moonlight!" Instead he sped an express rider to find Rodney, who had left the Congress.

"Caesar Rodney," John Adams described him, "is the oddest-looking man in the world; he is tall, thin and slender as a reed, pale; his face is not bigger than a large apple, yet there is a sense and fire, spirit, wit and humor in his countenance." There was also death in it. Suffering from skin cancer, he never appeared without a green scarf wrapped around his head to conceal his disease.

Intercepted on the way home by the express rider who told him how things stood at the Congress, Rodney immediately turned his horse and rode all night through a thunderstorm. His torturous eighty-mile ride was doubly heroic because, apart from the pain it cost him, he knew that his vote for Independence would end all hope of being able to seek medical aid in England. Arriving bone-tired, splashed with mud from head to foot, he wiped it off his haggard face as he entered the State House, supported by McKean, in time to swing Delaware's vote for freedom.

On the fateful day of July 2, 1776, as the delegates reassembled, Thomas Jefferson took temperature readings in the State House with a new thermometer he had bought. He found that at 9 a.m. it was already 78 degrees, and noted that the readings grew worse with the increasing heat and humidity.

The radicals had worked hard most of the night to convince the holdouts. Many who were finally persuaded to vote for Independence did not really approve of it. "There were several who signed with regret," John Adams wrote later, "and several others with many doubts and much lukewarmness."

Pressure on James Wilson finally swung Pennsylvania into the liberty column, and that on Edward Rutledge brought South Carolina over to the radicals. North Carolina was almost lost when Joseph Hewes turned against Independence, until John Adams alarmed him by warning of the wrath he would face from the majority of people in his colony, who favored it.

Surrendering, Hewes threw up his hands in despair and cried gloomily, "Then it is done! And I will abide by it."

New York abstained again for lack of instruction, but delegate Henry Wisner promised his colony would not stand apart, joining the other twelve when they received official word.

So the vote for Independence was unanimous.

It was a tremendous victory for the radicals, but John Adams saw it as a greater victory for all Americans.

"Yesterday the greatest question was decided which ever was debated in America," he wrote Abigail on July 3, "and a greater, perhaps, never was nor will be decided among men. . . . You will see in a few days a Declaration setting forth the causes which have impelled us to this mighty revolution, and the reasons which will justify it in the sight of God and man. . . . I am well aware of the toil and blood and treasure it will cost us to maintain this declaration and support and defend these States. Yet through all the gloom I can see the rays of ravishing light and glory."

A three-day debate began over the wording of the Declaration of Independence, which would now serve as the cornerstone of the new nation that had come into being. One delegate after another rose to raise angry objections to certain words or clauses, or protest the absence of others.

It was not easy for rich conservatives to swallow some of Jefferson's language—especially the idea that "all men are created equal," and that all had an equal right to "life, liberty and the pursuit of happiness." They vastly preferred the slogan of Sam Adams: "Life, liberty and property."

Out of the 1,800 words Jefferson had written, a quarter of them were slashed away in eighty-six changes. Agonized at this attack on his carefully wrought masterpiece, its author squirmed in glum silence. It was John Adams who jumped up persistently to protest, banging his cane furiously on the floor. But change after change was made in the interests of harmony.

Tempers were rubbed raw, not only by the debate, accusations, and counter-accusations, but also by the intolerably humid July heat. Horseflies entering the open windows from a neighboring stable forced the exasperated delegates to slap their bitten hands and stockinged legs.

The biggest fight broke out over Jefferson's attack on slavery in the Declaration. He had indicted the King for waging "cruel war against human nature itself, violating its most sacred rights of life and liberty in the persons of a distant people who never offended him, captivating and carrying them into slavery in another hemisphere, or to incur miserable death in their transportation . . . suppressing every legislative attempt to prohibit or restrain this execrable commerce."

The fight against this clause was led by South Carolina's Edward Rutledge, for whom the slavery issue was extremely delicate. In his colony four-fifths of the population was black. For that matter, almost one in every five Americans in 1776 was black, and most members of Congress owned slaves.

Rutledge argued that since nobody had *forced* Americans to take slaves, how could King George be blamed for it? Furthermore, didn't Washington and Hancock keep slaves themselves?

John Adams replied passionately that it was a mockery to talk of freedom in the Declaration, and yet say nothing of the lack of it for black Americans. Rutledge, whom Adams called "a peacock— excessively vain, excessively weak," scathingly denounced New England hypocrisy. Didn't their own schoonermasters make fat profits out of the slave trade?

Speaking for South Carolina and supported by the Georgia delegation, he warned that if all references to slavery were not removed, they would refuse to sign the Declaration.

"If we give in on this issue, there will be trouble a hundred years hence," Sam Adams warned grimly, remarkably prophesying the Civil War. "Posterity will never forgive us!"

But John Hancock told the Congress, "We must be unanimous—there must be no pulling different ways. We must all hang together." Benjamin Franklin added dryly, "We must indeed all hang together—or most assuredly we will all hang separately!"

The Congress finally removed the slavery paragraph to placate the Southern colonies and hold them in the Union.

Protesting this injustice to black Americans, Jefferson predicted, "Nothing is more certainly written in the Book of Fate than that this people shall be free. . . . The rights of human nature are deeply wounded by this infamous practice."

Finally, on the evening of the Fourth of July, debate was closed and all members present in the State House prepared to sign the Declaration of Independence. Thomas Jefferson wryly suggested later that they had done so only to escape the heat, the bothersome horseflies and the endless oratory.

First to sign was John Hancock. With a great flourish of his quill, he signed his name to the parchment document on his mahogany desk in bold, large strokes. "There!" he declared ostentatiously. "John Bull can read my name without spectacles, and may now double his reward of 500 pounds for my head. *That* is my defiance!" His huge signature gave the language a new slang term for anyone's signature—a "John Hancock."

John Adams wrote Abby, "I can see that the end is worth all the means. This is our day of deliverance. With solemn acts of devotion to God we ought to commemorate it. With pomp and parade, with shows, games, sports, guns, bells, bonfires and illuminations from one end of the continent to the other from this time forward evermore."

When the Declaration was first proclaimed in the State House yard at noon on Monday, July 8, in the presence of thirty-nine signers, a huge crowd roared in excitement. The liberty bell tolled, people paraded, bonfires blazed at night. Post riders galloped with copies north and south, electrifying every town and hamlet with the news.

"This Declaration has had a glorious effect," enthused New Hampshire official William Whipple. "It has made these colonies all alive!"

Washington had it read to his assembled troops at 6 p.m. on July 9, adding solemnly that the peace and safety of their new country depended now "solely on the success of our arms." Then he raised a hastily created new flag of the United Colonies—thirteen aternating red and white stripes with the crosses of St. Andrew and St. George, adapted, ironically, from the insignia of the British East India Tea Company.

Abigail Adams heard the Declaration read from the Boston State House balcony ten days later. "The bells rang," she wrote her husband, "the privateers fired the forts and batteries, the cannon were discharged, the platoons followed and every face appeared joyful. . . . After dinner the King's arms were taken down from the State House and every vestige of him from every place in which it appeared, and burned. . . . Thus ends royal authority in this State, and all the people shall say Amen."

The United States of America had been born.

FOURTEEN

The Fifty-Six Who Signed

Many names on the Declaration were signed after July 4, 1776, because those delegates were not members of the Congress, or were absent, at the time. To discourage the planting of spies or traitors in their midst, the Congress secretly ruled that no new delegate should be allowed to take a seat in the Congress that year until he had signed the Declaration.

New York's four new delegates did not reach the Congress until July 9. Last to sign was Delaware's Thomas McKean, who could not do so until January 1777 because after getting Rodney back to vote their colony for Independence, he had to rush off to lead a regiment to fight beside Washington.

Pennsylvania named a new delegation on July 20, leaving out forty-four-year-old John Dickinson, who had refused to sign on principle. He nevertheless told the Congress that he would support its decision, and proved it by promptly enlisting in the Continental Army as a private, even though he was a ranking Colonel in the Pennsylvania militia.

Not all of the signers were American-born. Ireland had sent Matthew Thornton, George Taylor, and James Smith. From Scotland came James Wilson and Dr. John Witherspoon. English-born were Robert Morris and Button Gwinnett. Francis Lewis came from Wales. There were no Quakers or Jews among the signers. Only one Catholic signed—Irish-descended Charles Carroll of Carrollton, Maryland, the richest man in America of that day, and one so zealous in the cause that the Crown had marked him out for special vengeance. Another Maryland signer, lawyer William Paca, came from Italian forebears.

Far from being all heroic figures, the signers ran the gamut from men of distinction and accomplishment to those who did little more than fill up space. Small, rapid-speaking Francis Hopkinson of New Jersey was a talented composer, and also designed the first flag of the United States. Connecticut judge Roger Sherman, who often sat apart from other delegates, sipping coffee from a bowl, had taught himself law while working at a cobbler's bench.

Virginia's mammoth Benjamin Harrison was, according to John Adams, an "indolent, luxurious, heavy gentleman of no use in Congress or committee, but a great embarrassment to both."

Rhode Island's shrewd Stephen Hopkins, the second oldest signer, was known as "Old Grape and Guts" because of his fondness for rum. He loved to sit up all night over a mug and conversation if he could get anybody to join him.

New Jersey's Abraham Clark was a self-educated surveyor and county sheriff who wrote a friend wryly about his new status as a signer: "As to my title, I know not yet whether it will be honorable or dishonorable; the issue of the war must settle it. Perhaps our Congress will be exalted on a high gallows."

Although the Declaration itself was released almost immediately, the Congress withheld the names of those signing it for six months to avoid delivering them to the hangman if the resistance collapsed. The only name revealed until then was that of John Hancock, who had to sign as President of the Congress to give the Declaration the force of a legal decree, and who was already an outlaw with a price on his head.

Not until January 18, 1777, was an official copy of the Declaration, with all its signatures, sent to each of the thirteen states. Then all Americans learned that the fifty-six of their fellow citizens who had signed were, by colonies:

Massachusetts Bay
John Hancock, 39, merchant; b. Braintree
Samuel Adams, 54, politician; b. Boston
John Adams, 41, lawyer; b. Braintree
Robert Treat Paine, 45, minister, jurist; b. Boston
Elbridge Gerry, 32, merchant; b. Marblehead

New Hampshire
Josiah Bartlett, 47, doctor, lawyer; b. Amesbury, Mass.
William Whipple, 46, merchant, jurist; b. Kittery, Me.
Matthew Thornton, 62, doctor, jurist; b. Ireland

Connecticut
Roger Sherman, 55, lawyer; b. Newton, Mass.
Samuel Huntington, 45, jurist; b. Windham County
William Williams, 45, merchant, jurist; b. Lebanon
Oliver Wolcott, 50, jurist, b. Windsor

Rhode Island
Stephen Hopkins, 69, merchant, jurist; b. Providence
William Ellery, 49, jurist; b. Providence

New York
William Floyd, 42, soldier; b. Brookhaven
Philip Livingston, 60, merchant; b. Albany
Francis Lewis, 63, merchant; b. Landaff, Wales

Lewis Morris, 50, farmer; b. Morrisania (N.Y.C.)

New Jersey

Richard Stockton, 46, lawyer; b. near Princeton
John Witherspoon, 53, educator; b. Gifford, Scotland
Francis Hopkinson, 39, jurist, musician; b. Philadelphia, Pa.
John Hart, 65 (?), farmer; b. Stonington, Conn.
Abraham Clark, 50, lawyer, financier; b. Elizabeth

Pennsylvania

Robert Morris, 42, merchant; b. Liverpool, England
Benjamin Rush, 31, doctor; b. Byberry (Philadelphia)
Benjamin Franklin, 70, printer, inventor; b. Boston, Mass.
John Morton, 52, jurist; b. Ridley
George Clymer, 37, merchant; b. Philadelphia
James Smith, 63, lawyer; b. Dublin, Ireland
George Taylor, 60, ironmonger; b. Ireland
James Wilson, 34, jurist; b. Carskerdo, Scotland
George Ross, 46, jurist; b. New Castle, Del.

Delaware

Caesar Rodney, 48, jurist; b. Dover
George Read, 43, jurist; b. near Northeast
Thomas McKean, 42, lawyer; b. New London, Pa.

Maryland

Samuel Chase, 35, jurist; b. Princess Anne
William Paca, 36, jurist; b. Abingdon
Thomas Stone, 33, lawyer; b. Charles County
Charles Carroll of Carrollton, 39, lawyer; b. Annapolis

Virginia

George Wythe, 50, lawyer; b. Elizabeth City
Richard Henry Lee, 44, farmer; b. Stratford
Thomas Jefferson, 33, lawyer; b. Old Shadwell
Benjamin Harrison, 50, farmer; b. Berkeley
Thomas Nelson, Jr., 38, soldier; b. Yorktown
Francis Lightfoot Lee, 42, farmer; b. Stratford
Carter Braxton, 40, farmer; b. King & Queen C.H.

North Carolina

William Hooper, 34, lawyer; b. Boston, Mass.
Joseph Hewes, 46, merchant; b. Kingston, N.J.
John Penn, 35, lawyer; b. near Port Royal, Va.

South Carolina

Edward Rutledge, 27, lawyer; b. Charleston
Thomas Heyward, Jr., 30, lawyer, farmer; b. St. Luke's Parish
Thomas Lynch, Jr., 27, farmer; b. Winyah
Arthur Middleton, 34, farmer; b. Charleston

Georgia

Button Gwinnett, 44, merchant; b. Down Hatherly, England
Lyman Hall, 52, doctor, jurist; b. Wallingford, Conn.
George Walton, 35, jurist; b. Prince Edward County, Va.

FIFTEEN

What Happened to the Men and Women of '76?

The moment the Declaration of Independence was signed, all leading American patriots became candidates for the King's gallows as traitors to the Crown. Not a single signer was hanged, however, although some had narrow squeaks and others underwent harrowing experiences.

The Redcoats failed to lay hands on Richard Henry Lee, who died a natural death at sixty-three, but his two young sons at school in England, unable to return, were horrified by being informed that their father was about to be hanged.

Although rich John Dickinson refused to sign the Declaration, his enlistment in the Continental Army as a private marked him for execution. "Johnny, you will be hanged," his anguished mother wept, "your estate will be forfeited and confiscated, you will leave your excellent wife a widow, and your charming children orphans, beggars and infamous!"

He escaped both being killed in battle and on the gallows, but the Pennsylvania legislature refused to return him to the Congress because his principles would not allow him to sign the Declaration. He protested bitterly, "While I was exposing my person to every hazard and lodging every night within half a mile of the enemy, the members of the Convention in Pennsylvania, resting in quiet safety, unanimously voted me unworthy of my seat!" Switching his allegiance to Delaware, he became a delegate for that state instead and contributed importantly to the writing of the Constitution.

John Morton's closest friends, Tories all, never forgave him for joining with Franklin and James Wilson to swing Pennsylvania to the side of Independence. Jurist Morton became the first signer to die, less than a year afterward. Heartbroken by the desertion of his friends, he left a poignant deathbed message for them: "Tell them that they will live to see the hour when they shall acknowledge it to have been the most glorious service that I ever rendered my country!"

Fifteen signers of the Declaration had their homes destroyed by the British, and many were broken in health by relentless pursuit or capture. Hessian troops laid to waste the farm, home, and mills of elderly John Hart of New Jersey in the winter of 1776. He managed to escape into the mountains, but his ordeals as a hunted fugitive left him so badly crippled that he died three years later.

New York merchant Francis Lewis had his home invaded and burned, and all his business properties seized. The British captured his wife, treating her so brutally that she died.

Tall, dignified Richard Stockton of New Jersey was captured late in 1776 by the British, who looted his home and burned his library. He was thrown into jail and tortured until he agreed to renounce the rebel cause. Shunned by his fellow Americans for his defection, he died a lonely, embittered invalid before the war was ended.

Button Gwinnett was killed eleven months after the Declaration when, as acting Governor of Georgia, he died in a duel with a general who called him a lying scoundrel. Ironically, although he died penniless, so few of his autographs survived him that one of his signatures later sold for $50,000.

The signer who died youngest was Thomas Lynch, Jr., of South Carolina, who was lost at sea in 1779 at age thirty.

Caesar Rodney, who became Governor of Delaware for most of the Revolution, lived for eight years after his historic all-night ride. He also led the Delaware militia against the British when they invaded his state. Struggling all the while with the skin cancer beneath his facial bandage, he finally succumbed to it in 1784.

History played ironic tricks on two signers. That "great embarrassment" to the Congress, fat Virginian Benjamin Harrison, won a claim to fame by becoming the progenitor of two American Presidents—son William Henry Harrison ("Tippecanoe and Tyler too") (1841) and great-grandson Benjamin Harrison (1889–93).

On the other hand, the name of stern-faced Elbridge Gerry became famous not as staunch patriot, signer, or Vice President under Madison, but for manipulating election districts as Governor of Massachusetts in order to ensure victory at the polls— the political trick we call "gerrymandering."

Edward Rutledge, despised by John Adams as an elegant "peacock," fought and was captured in the fall of Charlestown. Released in a prisoner exchange, he eventually became Governor of South Carolina.

Last survivor of all the signers was Charles Carroll of Carrollton, who died in 1832 at the age of ninety-five, four years after opening the Baltimore & Ohio Railroad—the only signer who lived long enough to see a locomotive.

And what of the principals of our drama?

In 1786 Sam Adams, now a respectable member of the Massachusetts State Council, was outraged when mobs of poor farmers, seeking to stop their property from being seized for debts, used violence to prevent the courts from sitting. He angrily proposed to hang anyone who dared resort to the rebellious methods he had used so shrewdly and successfully in 1774. Becoming Governor twenty years later, he died in 1803 at the age of eighty-one.

Benjamin Franklin was seventy when Congress sent him to France to get a military alliance. Lending the Congress three thousand pounds of his own money, he sighed there was little left of him now but "you may have me for what you please." He was tremendously popular in France, the darling of the ladies especially.

John Adams, who joined Benjamin in France, grew jealous of his popularity, writing peevishly to Abby that Benjamin was "possessed by the lowest cunning and deepest hypocrisy I have ever met." But Benjamin guaranteed the success of the Revolution by winning a French treaty that lent the Americans an army, navy, and five million dollars. He stayed on as Minister to France.

When Jefferson was sent overseas to relieve the tired old sage, the French Minister said, "You replace Dr. Franklin, I hear." Jefferson shook his head. "I succeed him, sir," he corrected. "No one can replace him."

In 1787 when eighty-one-year-old Benjamin entered the Constitutional Convention in Philadelphia, Washington suggested that the delegates give him a standing ovation—and they did.

Just before his death at eighty-four, Benjamin was asked to define his religious beliefs. With a little smile he replied that he no longer troubled to ponder about them, since he would shortly be finding out the answers for sure.

John Hancock finally achieved his yearning for military action in 1778 when he was made major general of the Massachusetts militia, only to fail miserably in trying to capture the British base at Rhode Island. But he presented a banner to a black military company under him called the Bucks of America, in tribute to their courage and devotion in action.

When the Revolution was finally won, Hancock wrote in November 1783, "I have for ten years past devoted myself to the concern of the Public. . . . I have lost many thousand sterling but, thank God, my country is saved and by the smile of heaven I am a free and independent man." He died ten years later.

Martha Washington proved a great comfort not only to her husband George, but also to his troops. Sharing the hard winter with them at Valley Forge, she did all she could to relieve their misery. At a spring rally when news of the French Alliance was read, a soldier shouted, "Long live Lady Washington!" and the valley rang with enthusiastic cheers.

When George was President, he and Martha invited a unique visitor—Deborah Samson, who had served in men's clothes in the Continental Army. Soon afterwards Deborah, a widow with three children, fell on hard times. Paul Revere lent her money and won her a soldier's pension—the princely sum of four dollars a month. This was seventy cents more a month than the pension paid by the Pennsylvania legislature to another woman hero, Molly Pitcher.

George Washington's accomplishments as President scarcely need elaboration. George refused to serve three terms, grateful to be allowed to retire with Martha to their beloved Mount Vernon. At peace at last for two years, he died at sixty-nine in December 1799, two weeks before the dawn of the nineteenth century. Life was so empty without him that Martha sighed to a minister she would "welcome the time when she should be called to follow." She was called thirty months later.

One day after the signing of the Declaration, Patrick Henry took the oath of office as first Governor of the new Commonwealth of Virginia. In 1778 he helped expose a plot to remove Washington from command of the Continental Army. Three years later he fell out with Jefferson over political differences, and their feud lasted a lifetime. A leader in the fight for adoption of the Bill of Rights, he was principally responsible for making it part of the Constitution. In his old age, ironically, he turned crustily conservative. When he died at sixty-six he was vastly unpopular with fellow Virginians who had once hailed him as their fearless spokesman for rebellion.

Honest John Adams once confessed that, at any point during the Revolution, he would have given everything he owned if it could somehow have been magically erased, and the old colonial system restored. Thomas Jefferson too, had second thoughts about the wisdom of the Declaration. Even two months after he had written it, he wrote his kinsman John Randolph that he was "looking with fondness towards a reconciliation with Great Britain." Both men reflected common doubts of 1776.

John Adams was separated from his wife for six years when he was sent to Europe to help negotiate the peace treaty in 1783 and serve as Minister to England. Abby finally joined him overseas for four years, manifesting Puritanical distaste for sophisticated British and French society.

When John became President in 1797, he and Abby suffered public abuse. Abby was called "Mrs. President" because of her strong influence over John's decisions. She was blamed more than he for the Alien and Sedition Acts of 1798 that were intended primarily to silence the critical press. The Acts, and John's insistence upon the supremacy of federal over state power, led him to feud bitterly with Thomas Jefferson.

When Jefferson defeated him for the Presidency in 1800, John retired with Abby to their home in Quincy. The tranquility of retirement did not appeal to the bustling Abby, who wrote her sister, "I have frequently said to my friends, when they have thought me overburdened with care, I would rather have too much than too little. Life stagnates without action. I could never bear merely to vegetate."

She died in 1816, an active, alert seventy-two.

Almost as soon as the Declaration had been signed, Thomas Jefferson rushed home to his beloved Martha. Refusing to leave her again for Philadelphia, he served in the Virginia legislature and in 1779 succeeded Patrick Henry as Governor. When the British prepared to invade defenseless Richmond, the capital, Thomas rushed Martha and the children to safety and only escaped capture himself by a margin of five minutes.

Childbirth in 1782 seriously weakened the ailing Martha, who became bedridden. Knowing that she was dying, her anguished husband spent every moment he could at her side. When she died quietly at age thirty-four, he tried to conceal his grief from the world because it was too private, too deep.

Still inconsolable three years later, he was asked if he would consider going to France as American Minister. He replied quietly, "I would go to hell to serve my country." In France he observed and sympathized with the French Revolution.

Becoming Washington's Secretary of State, he resigned in protest against Alexander Hamilton's policies, and became the leader of the new Democratic-Republican (today's Democratic) party. As Vice President under John Adams, he feuded with him too, and defeated him for the Presidency in 1800.

When he went to the White House, the role of First Lady was filled by his daughter Patsy. He never married again.

As President he vastly increased American territory through the Louisiana Purchase in 1803, and sent the Lewis and Clark expedition to explore the Northwest. After two terms he returned home to found the University of Virginia in 1819 and influence a revival of classical architecture.

Both Thomas Jefferson, retired in Monticello, and John Adams, retired in Quincy, lived long enough to be invited to the White House by Adams' son, John Quincy Adams, for the 50th anniversary celebration of the Declaration of Independence.

By that time all the other principals in the Revolutionary drama were dead—Sam Adams, Abby Adams, Benjamin Franklin, John Hancock, Martha Jefferson, George Washington, Martha Washington, Patrick Henry, Thomas Paine, Richard Henry Lee, Caesar Rodney, Elbridge Gerry, Edward Rutledge.

The two old Revolutionary comrades—John now ninety-one, Thomas eighty-three—had by this time mellowed sufficiently to patch up their bitter quarrel by correspondence. But neither was well enough to go to the White House to shake hands at the celebration, although each assumed the other had gone.

Instead, in one of the most remarkable coincidences in American history, Thomas Jefferson and John Adams both died on that very same day—the Fourth of July, 1826, fiftieth anniversary of the Declaration of Independence that both had labored so valiantly together to achieve.

7/17-3
11/19 - 3 (7/17)